THE DAILY STUDY BIBLE SERIES
REVISED EDITION

THE LETTERS TO THE
PHILIPPIANS, COLOSSIANS,
AND
THESSALONIANS

THE LETTERS TO THE
PHILIPPIANS, COLOSSIANS,
AND
THESSALONIANS

REVISED EDITION

Translated
with an Introduction and Interpretation
by
WILLIAM BARCLAY

THE WESTMINSTER PRESS
PHILADELPHIA

Revised Edition
Copyright © 1975 William Barclay

First published by The Saint Andrew Press
Edinburgh, Scotland

Philippians, First Edition, 1957; Second Edition, 1959

Colossians, First Edition, 1957; Second Edition, 1959

I and II Thessalonians, First Edition, 1954; Second Edition, 1959

Published by The Westminster Press ®
Philadelphia, Pennsylvania

PRINTED IN THE UNITED STATES OF AMERICA

3   4   5   6   7

Library of Congress Cataloging in Publication Data

Bible. N.T. Epistles of Paul. English. Barclay.
    1975.
    The letters to the Philippians, Colossians, and
Thessalonians.

    (The Daily study Bible series. — Rev. ed.)
    1. Bible. N.T. Philippians — Commentaries.
2. Bible. N.T. Colossians — Commentaries.
3. Bible. N.T. Thessalonians — Commentaries.
I. Barclay, William, lecturer in the University
of Glasgow. II. Title. III. Series.
BS2643.B37   1975   227   75-26525
ISBN 0-664-21310-3
ISBN 0-664-24110-7 pbk.

GENERAL INTRODUCTION

The Daily Study Bible series has always had one aim—to convey the results of scholarship to the ordinary reader. A. S. Peake delighted in the saying that he was a "theological middleman", and I would be happy if the same could be said of me in regard to these volumes. And yet the primary aim of the series has never been academic. It could be summed up in the famous words of Richard of Chichester's prayer—to enable men and women "to know Jesus Christ more clearly, to love him more dearly, and to follow him more nearly".

It is all of twenty years since the first volume of *The Daily Study Bible* was published. The series was the brain-child of the late Rev. Andrew McCosh, M.A., S.T.M., the then Secretary and Manager of the Committee on Publications of the Church of Scotland, and of the late Rev. R. G. Macdonald, O.B.E., M.A., D.D., its Convener.

It is a great joy to me to know that all through the years *The Daily Study Bible* has been used at home and abroad, by minister, by missionary, by student and by layman, and that it has been translated into many different languages. Now, after so many printings, it has become necessary to renew the printer's type and the opportunity has been taken to restyle the books, to correct some errors in the text and to remove some references which have become outdated. At the same time, the Biblical quotations within the text have been changed to use the Revised Standard Version, but my own original translation of the New Testament passages has been retained at the beginning of each daily section.

There is one debt which I would be sadly lacking in courtesy if I did not acknowledge. The work of revision and correction has been done entirely by the Rev. James Martin, M.A., B.D., minister of High Carntyne Church, Glasgow. Had it not been for him this task would never have been undertaken, and it is impossible for me to thank him enough for the selfless toil he has put into the revision of these books.

It is my prayer that God may continue to use *The Daily Study Bible* to enable men better to understand His word.

Glasgow   WILLIAM BARCLAY

CONTENTS

COLOSSIANS

CONTENTS

1 THESSALONIANS

CONTENTS

2 THESSALONIANS

A GENERAL INTRODUCTION
TO THE LETTERS OF PAUL

THE LETTERS OF PAUL

There is no more interesting body of documents in the New Testament than the letters of Paul. That is because of all forms of literature a letter is most personal. Demetrius, one of the old Greek literary critics, once wrote, "Every one reveals his own soul in his letters. In every other form of composition it is possible to discern the writer's character, but in none so clearly as the epistolary." (Demetrius, *On Style,* 227). It is just because he left us so many letters that we feel we know Paul so well. In them he opened his mind and heart to the folk he loved so much; and in them, to this day, we can see that great mind grappling with the problems of the early church, and feel that great heart throbbing with love for men, even when they were misguided and mistaken.

THE DIFFICULTY OF LETTERS

At the same time, there is often nothing so difficult to understand as a letter. Demetrius (*On Style,* 223) quotes a saying of Artemon, who edited the letters of Aristotle. Artemon said that a letter ought to be written in the same manner as a dialogue, because it was one of the two sides of a dialogue. In other words, to read a letter is like listening to one side of a telephone conversation. So when we read the letters of Paul we are often in a difficulty. We do not possess the letter which he was answering; we do not fully know the circumstances with which he was dealing; it is only from the letter itself that we can deduce the situation which prompted it. Before we can hope to understand fully any letter Paul wrote, we must try to reconstruct the situation which produced it.

THE ANCIENT LETTERS

It is a great pity that Paul's letters were ever called *epistles.* They are in the most literal sense *letters.* One of the great lights shed on the interpretation of the New Testament has been the discovery and the publication of the *papyri*. In the ancient world, *papyrus* was the substance on which most documents were written. It was composed of strips of the pith of a certain bulrush that grew on the banks of the Nile. These strips were laid one on top of the other to form a substance very like brown paper. The sands of the Egyptian desert were ideal for preservation, for papyrus, although very brittle, will last forever so long as moisture does not get at it. As a result, from the Egyptian rubbish heaps, archaeologists have rescued hundreds of documents, marriage contracts, legal agreements, government forms, and, most interesting of all, private letters. When we read these private letters we find that there was a pattern to which nearly all conformed; and we find that Paul's letters reproduce exactly that pattern. Here is one of these ancient letters. It is from a soldier, called Apion, to his father Epimachus. He is writing from Misenum to tell his father that he has arrived safely after a stormy passage.

"Apion sends heartiest greetings to his father and lord Epimachus. I pray above all that you are well and fit; and that things are going well with you and my sister and her daughter and my brother. I thank my Lord Serapis [his god] that he kept me safe when I was in peril on the sea. As soon as I got to Misenum I got my journey money from Caesar—three gold pieces. And things are going fine with me. So I beg you, my dear father, send me a line, first to let me know how you are, and then about my brothers, and thirdly, that I may kiss your hand, because you brought me up well, and because of that I hope, God willing, soon to be promoted. Give Capito my heartiest greetings, and my brothers and Serenilla and my friends. I sent you a little picture of myself painted by Euctemon. My military name is Antonius Maximus. I pray for your good health. Serenus sends good wishes, Agathos Daimon's boy, and Turbo, Gallonius's son." (G. Milligan, *Selections from the Greek Papyri,* 36).

Little did Apion think that we would be reading his letter to his father 1800 years after he had written it. It shows how little human nature changes. The lad is hoping for promotion quickly. Who will Serenilla be but the girl he left behind him? He sends the ancient equivalent of a photograph to the folk at home. Now that letter falls into certain sections. (i) There is a greeting. (ii) There is a prayer for the health of the recipients. (iii) There is a thanksgiving to the gods. (iv) There are the special contents. (v) Finally, there are the special salutations and the personal greetings. Practically every one of Paul's letters shows exactly the same sections, as we now demonstrate.

(i) *The Greeting: Romans* 1: 1; 1 *Corinthians* 1: 1; 2 *Corinthians* 1: 1; *Galatians* 1: 1; *Ephesians* 1.: 1; *Philippians* 1: 1; *Colossians* 1: 1, 2; 1 *Thessalonians* 1: 1; 2 *Thessalonians* 1: 1.

(ii) *The Prayer:* in every case Paul prays for the grace of God on the people to whom he writes: *Romans* 1: 7; 1 *Corinthians* 1: 3; 2 *Corinthians* 1: 2; *Galatians* 1: 3; *Ephesians* 1: 2; *Philippians* 1: 3; *Colossians* 1: 2; 1 *Thessalonians* 1: 1; 2 *Thessalonians* 1: 2.

(iii) *The Thanksgiving: Romans* 1: 8; 1 *Corinthians* 1: 4; 2 *Corinthians* 1: 3; *Ephesians* 1: 3; *Philippians* 1: 3; 1 *Thessalonians* 1: 3; 2 *Thessalonians* 1: 3.

(iv) *The Special Contents:* the main body of the letters.

(v) *Special Salutations and Personal Greetings: Romans* 16; 1 *Corinthians* 16: 19; 2 *Corinthians* 13: 13; *Philippians* 4: 21, 22; *Colossians* 4: 12–15; 1 *Thessalonians* 5: 26.

When Paul wrote letters, he wrote them on the pattern which everyone used. Deissmann says of them, "They differ from the messages of the homely papyrus leaves of Egypt, not as letters but only as the letters of Paul." When we read Paul's letters we are not reading things which were meant to be academic exercises and theological treatises, but human documents written by a friend to his friends.

THE IMMEDIATE SITUATION

With a very few exceptions, all Paul's letters were written to meet an immediate situation and not treatises which he sat down to write in the peace and silence of his study. There was some threatening situation in Corinth, or Galatia, or Philippi, or Thessalonica, and he wrote a letter to meet it. He was not in the least thinking of us when he wrote, but solely of the people to whom he was writing. Deissmann writes, "Paul had no thought of adding a few fresh compositions to the already extant Jewish epistles; still less of enriching the sacred literature of his nation. . . . He had no presentiment of the place his words would occupy in universal history; not so much that they would be in existence in the next generation, far less that one day people would look at them as Holy Scripture." We must always remember that a thing need not be transient because it was written to meet an immediate situation. All the great love songs of the world were written for one person, but they live on for the whole of mankind. It is just because Paul's letters were written to meet a threatening danger or a clamant need that they still throb with life. And it is because human need and the human situation do not change that God speaks to us through them today.

THE SPOKEN WORD

One other thing we must note about these letters. Paul did what most people did in his day. He did not normally pen his own letters but dictated them to a secretary, and then added his own authenticating signature. (We actually know the name of one of the people who did the writing for him. In *Romans* 16: 22 Tertius, the secretary, slips in his own greeting before the letter draws to an end). In 1 *Corinthians* 16: 21 Paul says, "This is my own signature, my autograph, so that you can be sure this letter comes from me." (cp. *Colossians* 4: 18; 2 *Thessalonians* 3: 17.)

This explains a great deal. Sometimes Paul is hard to understand, because his sentences begin and never finish; his grammar breaks down and the construction becomes involved. We must not think of him sitting quietly at a desk, carefully polishing each sentence as he writes. We must think of him striding up and down some little room, pouring out a torrent of words, while his secretary races to get them down. When Paul composed his letters, he had in his mind's eye a vision of the folk to whom he was writing, and he was pouring out his heart to them in words that fell over each other in his eagerness to help.

THE LETTER TO THE PHILIPPIANS

INTRODUCTION TO THE LETTER TO
THE PHILIPPIANS

WE are fortunate in one thing in our study of *Philippians*—there are practically no critical problems involved; for no reputable New Testament critic has ever doubted its genuineness. We can accept *Philippians* as undoubtedly an authentic letter of Paul.

PHILIPPI

When Paul chose a place wherein to preach the gospel, he always did so with the eye of a strategist. He always chose one which was not only important in itself but was also the key point of a whole area. To this day many of Paul's preaching-centres are still great road centres and railway junctions. Such was Philippi which had at least three great claims to distinction.

(i) In the neighbourhood there were gold and silver mines, which had been worked as far back as the time of the Phoenicians. It is true that by the time of the Christian era they had become exhausted, but they had made Philippi a great commercial centre of the ancient world.

(ii) The city had been founded by Philip, father of Alexander the Great, and it is his name that it bears. It was founded on the site of an ancient city called *Krēnidēs,* a name which means The Wells or Fountains. Philip had founded Philippi in 368 B.C. because there was no more strategic site in all Europe. There is a range of hills which divides Europe from Asia, east from west and just at Philippi that chain of hills dips into a pass so that the city commanded the road from Europe to Asia, since the road must go through the pass. This was the reason that one of the great battles of history was fought at Philippi; for it was here that Antony defeated Brutus and Cassius, and thereby decided the future of the Roman Empire.

(iii) Not very long after, Philippi attained the dignity of a Roman Colony. The Roman Colonies were amazing institutions. They were not colonies in the sense of being outposts of civilization in unexplored parts of the world. They had begun by having a military significance. It was the custom of Rome to send out parties of veteran soldiers, who had served their time and been granted citizenship, to settle in strategic road centres. Usually these parties consisted of three hundred veterans with their wives and children. These colonies were the focal points of the great Roman road systems which were so engineered that reinforcements could speedily be sent from one colony to another. They were founded to keep the peace and to command the strategic centres in Rome's far-flung Empire. At first they had been founded in Italy; but soon they were scattered throughout the whole Empire, as the Empire grew. In later days the title of colony was given by the government to any city which it wished to honour for faithful service.

Wherever they were, these colonies were little fragments of Rome and their pride in their Roman citizenship was their dominating characteristic. The Roman language was spoken; Roman dress was worn; Roman customs were observed; their magistrates had Roman titles, and carried out the same ceremonies as were carried out in Rome itself. They were stubbornly and unalterably Roman and would never have dreamt of becoming assimilated to the people amidst whom they were set. We can hear the Roman pride breathing through the charge against Paul and Silas in *Acts* 16: 20, 21: "These men are Jews, and they are trying to teach and to introduce laws and customs which it is not right for us to observe— *for we are Romans.*"

"You are a colony of heaven" (A.V.), Paul wrote to the Philippian Church (3: 20). Just as the Roman colonist never forgot in any environment that he was a Roman, so they must never forget in any society that they were Christians. Nowhere were men prouder of being Roman citizens than in these colonies; and such was Philippi.

PAUL AND PHILIPPI

It was on the second missionary journey, about the year

A.D. 52, that Paul first came to Philippi. Urged on by the vision of the man of Macedonia with his appeal to come over and help us, Paul had sailed from Alexandrian Troas in Asia Minor. He had landed at Neapolis in Europe, and thence made his way to Philippi.

The story of Paul's stay in Philippi is told in *Acts* 16; and an interesting story it is. It centres round three people— Lydia, the seller of purple; the demented slave-girl, used by her masters to tell fortunes; and the Roman gaoler. It is an extraordinary cross-section of ancient life. These three people were of different nationalities. Lydia was an *Asiatic*, and her name may well be not a proper name at all but simply "the Lydian lady." The slave-girl was a native *Greek*. The gaoler was a *Roman* citizen. The whole Empire was being gathered into the Christian Church. But not only were these three of different nationalities; they came from very different grades of society. Lydia was a dealer in purple, one of the most costly substances in the ancient world, and was the equivalent of a *merchant prince*. The girl was a *slave,* and, therefore, in the eyes of the law not a person at all, but a living tool. The gaoler was a Roman citizen, member of the sturdy Roman *middle-class* from which the civil service was drawn. In these three the top, the bottom and middle of society are all represented. No chapter in the Bible shows so well the all-embracing faith which Jesus Christ brought to men.

PERSECUTION

Paul had to leave Philippi after a storm of persecution and an illegal imprisonment. That persecution was inherited by the Philippian Church. He tells them that they have shared in his bonds and in his defence of the gospel (1: 7). He bids them not to fear their adversaries for they are going through what he himself has gone through and is now enduring (1: 28–30).

TRUE FRIENDSHIP

There had grown up between Paul and the Philippian Church

a bond of friendship closer than that which existed between him and any other Church. It was his proud boast that he had never taken help from any man or from any Church, and that, with his own two hands, he had satisfied his needs. It was from the Philippians alone that he had agreed to accept a gift. Soon after he left them and moved on to Thessalonica, they sent him a present (4: 16). When he moved on and arrived in Corinth by way of Athens, they alone again remembered him with their gifts (2 *Corinthians* 11: 9). "My brethren whom I love and long for," he calls them, "my joy and crown in the Lord" (4: 1).

THE OCCASION OF THE WRITING OF THE LETTER

When Paul wrote this letter he was in prison in Rome, and he wrote it with certain definite objects.

(i) It is a letter of thanks. The years have passed; it is now A.D. 63 or 64 and once again the Philippians have sent him a gift (4: 10, 11).

(ii) It has to do with Epaphroditus. It seems that the Philippians had sent him not only as a bearer of their gift, but that he might stay with Paul and be his personal servant. But Epaphroditus had fallen ill. He was sick for home; and he was worried because he knew that the people at home were worried about him. Paul sent him home, but he had the unhappy feeling that the people in Philippi might think Epaphroditus a quitter, so he goes out of his way to give him a testimonial: "Receive him with all joy, and honour such men, for he nearly died for the work of Christ" (2: 29, 30). There is something very moving in the sight of Paul, himself in prison and awaiting death, seeking to make things easier for Epaphroditus, when he was unexpectedly and unwillingly compelled to go home. Here is the peak of Christian courtesy.

(iii) It is a letter of encouragement to the Philippians in the trials which they are going through (1: 28–30).

(iv) It is an appeal for unity. It is from that, that there rises the great passage which speaks of the selfless humility of Jesus Christ (2: 1–11). In the Church at Philippi there were two women who had quarrelled and were endangering the peace

(4: 2); and there were false teachers who were seeking to lure the Philippians from the true path (3: 2). This letter is an appeal to maintain the unity of the Church.

THE PROBLEM

It is just here that the problem of *Philippians* arises. At 3: 2 there is an extraordinary break in the letter. Up to 3: 1 everything is serenity and the letter seems to be drawing gently to its close; then without warning comes the outburst: "Beware of dogs; beware of evil workers; beware of the concision." There is no connection with what goes before. Further, 3: 1 looks like the end. "Finally, my brethren," says Paul, "rejoice in the Lord" and having said *finally* he begins all over again! (That, of course, is not an unknown phenomenon in preaching).

Because of this break many scholars think that *Philippians,* as we possess it, is not one letter but two letters put together. They regard 3: 2–4: 3 as a letter of thanks and warning sent quite early after the arrival of Epaphroditus in Rome; and they regard 1: 1–3: 1 and 4: 4–4: 23 as a letter written a good deal later, and sent with Epaphroditus when he had to go home. That is perfectly possible. We know that Paul almost certainly did, in fact, write more than one letter to Philippi, for Polycarp, in his letter to the Philippian Church, says of him, "when he was absent he wrote *letters* to you."

THE EXPLANATION

And yet it seems to us that there is no good reason for splitting this letter into two. The sudden break between 3: 1 and 3: 2 can be otherwise explained in one of two ways.

(i) As Paul was writing, fresh news may have come of trouble at Philippi; and there and then he may have interrupted his line of thought to deal with it.

(ii) The simplest explanation is this. *Philippians* is a personal letter and a personal letter is never logically ordered like a treatise. In such a letter we put things down as they come into our heads; we chat on paper with our friends; and an association of ideas which may be clear enough to us may not be so obvious to anyone else. The sudden change of subject here is just the kind of thing which might occur in any such letter.

THE LOVELY LETTER

For many of us *Philippians* is the loveliest letter Paul ever wrote. It has been called by two titles. It has been called *The Epistle of Excellent Things*—and so indeed it is; and it has been called *The Epistle of Joy*. Again and again the words *joy* and *rejoice* recur. "Rejoice," writes Paul, "again I will say rejoice," even in prison directing the hearts of his friends—and ours— to the joy that no man can take from us.

PHILIPPIANS

A FRIEND TO HIS FRIENDS

Philippians 1: 1, 2

Paul and Timothy, slaves of Jesus Christ, write this letter to all those in Philippi who are consecrated to God because of their relationship to Jesus Christ, together with the overseers and the deacons.

Grace be to you and peace from God, our Father, and from the Lord Jesus Christ.

THE opening sentence sets the tone of the whole letter. It is characteristically a letter from a friend to his friends. With the exception of the letter to the Thessalonians and the little personal note to Philemon, Paul begins every letter with a statement of his apostleship; he begins, for instance, the letter to the Romans: "Paul a servant of Jesus Christ, *called to be an apostle*" (cp. 1 *Corinthians* 1: 1; 2 *Corinthians* 1: 1; *Galatians* 1: 1; *Ephesians* 1: 1; *Colossians* 1: 1). In the other letters he begins with a statement of his official position, why he has the right to write, and why the recipients have the duty to listen; but not when he writes to the Philippians. There is no need; he knows that they will listen, and listen lovingly. Of all his Churches, the Church at Philippi was the one to which Paul was closest; and he writes, not as an apostle to members of his Church, but as a friend to his friends.

Nonetheless, Paul does lay claim to one title. He claims to be the servant (*doulos*) of Christ, as the Authorized and Revised Standard Versions have it; but *doulos* is more than *servant*, it is *slave*. A servant is free to come and go; but a slave is the possession of his master for ever. When Paul calls himself the slave of Jesus Christ, he does three things. (i) He lays it down that he is the absolute possession of Christ. Christ has loved him and bought him with a price (1 *Corinthians* 6: 20), and he can never belong to anyone else. (ii) He lays it down that he owes an absolute obedience to Christ. The slave has no will of his own; his master's will must be his. So Paul has no will but Christ's, and no obedience but to his Saviour and Lord. (iii) In the Old Testament the regular title of the prophets is *the servants of God* (*Amos* 3: 7; *Jeremiah* 7: 25). That is the title which is given to Moses, to Joshua and to David (*Joshua* 1: 2; *Judges* 2: 8; *Psalm* 78: 70; 89: 3, 20). In fact, the highest of all titles of honour is *servant of God*; and when Paul takes this title, he humbly places himself in the succession of the prophets and of the great ones of God. The Christian's slavery to Jesus Christ is no cringing subjection. As the Latin tag has it: *Illi servire est regnare*, to be his slave is to be a king.

THE CHRISTIAN DISTINCTION

Philippians 1: 1, 2 (*continued*)

THE letter is addressed, as the Revised Standard Version has it, *to all the saints in Christ Jesus*. The word translated *saint* is *hagios*; and *saint* is a misleading translation. To modern ears it paints a picture of almost unworldly piety. Its connection is rather with stained glass windows than with the market-place. Although it is easy to see the meaning of *hagios* it is hard to translate it.

Hagios, and its Hebrew equivalent *kadosh*, are usually translated *holy*. In Hebrew thought, if a thing is described as *holy*, the basic idea is that it is *different* from other things; it is in some sense *set apart*. The better to understand this, let us look at how *holy* is actually used in the Old Testament. When the regulations regarding the priesthood are being laid down, it is written: "They shall be *holy* to their God" (*Leviticus* 21 : 6). The priests were to be *different* from other men, for they were set apart for a special function. The tithe was the tenth part of all produce which was to be set apart for God, and it is laid down: "The tenth shall be *holy* to the Lord, because it is the Lord's" (*Leviticus* 27: 30, 32). The tithe was *different* from other things which could be used as food. The central part of the Temple was the *Holy Place* (*Exodus* 26: 33); it was *different* from all other places. The word was specially used of the Jewish nation itself. The Jews were a *holy nation* (*Exodus* 19: 6). They were *holy* unto the Lord; God had severed them from other nations that they might be his (*Leviticus* 20: 26); it was they of all nations on the face of the earth whom God had specially known (*Amos* 3: 2). The Jews were different from all other nations, for they had a special place in the purpose of God.

But they refused to play the part which God meant them to play; when his Son came into the world, they failed to recognize him, and rejected and crucified him. The privileges and the responsibilities they should have had were taken away from the nation of Israel and given to the Church, which became the new Israel, the real people of God. Therefore, just as the Jews had once been *hagios, holy, different,* so now the Christians must be *hagios*; the Christians are the holy ones, the different ones, the *saints*. Thus Paul in his pre-Christian days was a notorious persecutor of the *saints,* the *hagioi* (*Acts* 9: 13); Peter goes to visit the *saints,* the *hagioi,* at Lydda (*Acts* 9: 32).

To say that the Christians are the saints means, therefore, that the Christians are *different* from other people. Wherein does that difference lie?

Paul addresses his people as saints *in Christ Jesus.* No one can read his letters without seeing how often the phrases *in Christ, in Christ Jesus, in the Lord* occur. *In Christ Jesus* occurs 48 times, *in Christ* 34 times, and *in the Lord* 50 times. Clearly this was for Paul the very essence of Christianity. What did he mean? Marvin R. Vincent says that when Paul spoke of the Christian being in Christ, he meat that the Christian lives in Christ as a bird in the air, a fish in the water, the roots of a tree in the soil. What makes the Christian different is that he is always and everywhere conscious of the encircling presence of Jesus Christ.

When Paul speaks of *the saints in Christ Jesus,* he means those who are different from other people and who are consecrated to God because of their special relationship to Jesus Christ—and that is what every Christian should be.

THE ALL-INCLUSIVE GREETING

Philippians 1: 1, 2 (*continued*)

PAUL'S greeting to his friends is: Grace be to you and peace, from God the Father, and from our Lord Jesus Christ (cp. *Romans* 1: 7; 1 *Corinthians* 1: 3; 2 *Corinthians* 1: 2; *Galatians* 1: 3; *Ephesians* 1: 2; *Colossians* 1: 2; 1 *Thessalonians* 1: 1; 2 *Thessalonians* 1: 2; *Philemon* 3).

When Paul put together these two great words, *grace* and *peace,* (*charis* and *eirēnē*), he was doing something very wonderful. He was taking the normal greeting phrases of two great nations and moulding them into one. *Charis* is the greeting with which Greek letters always began and *eirēnē* the greeting with which Jews met each other. Each of these words had its own flavour and each was deepened by the new meaning which Christianity poured into it.

Charis is a lovely word; the basic ideas in it are joy and pleasure, brightness and beauty; it is, in fact, connected with the English word *charm.* But with Jesus Christ there comes a new beauty to add to the beauty that was there. And that beauty is born of a new relationship to God. With Christ life becomes lovely because man is no longer the victim of God's law but the child of his love

Eirēnē is a comprehensive word. We translate it *peace*; but it never means a negative peace, never simply the absence of trouble. It means total well-being, everything that makes for a man's highest good.

It may well be connected with the Greek word *eirein,* which means *to join, to weave together.* And this peace has always got to do with personal relationships, a man's relationship to himself, to his fellow-men, and to God. It is always the peace that is born of reconciliation.

So, when Paul prays for grace and peace on his people he is praying that they should have the joy of knowing God as Father and the peace of being reconciled to God, to men, and to themselves—and that grace and peace can come only through Jesus Christ.

THE MARKS OF THE CHRISTIAN LIFE

(i) THE CHRISTIAN JOY

Philippians 1: 3–11

In all my remembrance of you I thank my God for you, and always in every one of my prayers, I pray for you with joy, because you have been in partnership with me for the furtherance of the gospel from the first day until now, and of this I am confident, that he who began a good work in you will complete it so that you may be ready for the day of Jesus Christ. And it is right for me to feel like this about you, because I have you in my heart, because all of you are partners in grace with me, both in my hands, and in my defence and confirmation of the gospel. God is my witness how I yearn for you all with the very compassion of Christ Jesus. And this I pray, that your love for each other may continue to abound more and more in all fulness of knowledge and in all sensitiveness of perception, that you may test the things which differ, that you may be yourselves pure and that you may cause no other to stumble, in preparation for the day of Christ, because you have been filled with the fruit which the righteousness which comes through Jesus Christ produces, and which issues in glory and praise to God.

IT is a lovely thing when, as Ellicott puts it, remembrance and gratitude are bound up together. In our personal relationships it is a great thing to have nothing but happy memories; and that was how Paul was with the Christians at Philippi. To remember brought no regrets, only happiness.

In this passage there are set out the marks of the Christian life.

There is *Christian joy*. It is with joy that Paul prays for his friends. The Letter to the Philippians has been called *The Epistle of Joy*. Bengel in his terse Latin commented: "*Summa epistolae gaudeo—gaudete.*" "The whole point of the letter is I do rejoice; do you rejoice." Let us look at the picture of Christian joy which this letter paints.

(i) In 1: 4 there is the joy of *Christian prayer*, the joy of bringing those we love to the mercy seat of God.

George Reindrop in his book *No Common Task* tells how a nurse once taught a man to pray and in doing so changed his whole life, until a dull, disgruntled and dispirited creature became a man of joy. Much of the nurse's work was done with her hands, and she used her hands as a scheme of prayer. Each finger stood for someone. Her thumb was nearest to her, and it reminded her to pray for those who were closest to her. The second finger was used for pointing and it stood for all her teachers in school and in the hospital. The third finger was the tallest and it stood for the V.I.P.s, the leaders in every sphere of life. The fourth finger was the weakest, as every pianist knows, and it stood for those who were in trouble and in pain. The little finger was the smallest and the least important and to the nurse it stood for herself.

There must always be a deep joy and peace in bringing our loved ones and others to God in prayer.

(ii) There is the joy that *Jesus Christ is preached* (1: 18). When a man enjoys a great blessing surely his first instinct must be to share it; and there is joy in thinking of the gospel being preached all over the world, so that another and another and another is brought within the love of Christ.

(iii) There is the joy of *faith* (1: 25). If Christianity does not make a man happy, it will not make him anything at all. There is a certain type of Christianity which is a tortured affair. The Psalmist said, "They looked to him and were radiant." When Moses came down from the mountain top his face shone. Christianity is the faith of the happy heart and the shining face.

(iv) There is the joy of seeing *Christians in fellowship together* (2: 2). As the Psalmist sang (*Psalm* 133: 1):

> Behold how good a thing it is,
> And how becoming well,
> Together such as brethren are
> In unity to dwell!

There is peace for no one where there are broken human relationships and strife between man and man. There is no lovelier sight than a family linked in love to each other or a Church whose members are one with each other because they are one in Christ Jesus their Lord.

(v) There is the joy of *suffering for Christ* (2: 17). In the hour of his martyrdom in the flames Polycarp prayed, "I thank thee, O Father, that thou hast judged me worthy of this hour." To suffer for Christ is a privilege, for it is an opportunity to demonstrate beyond mistake where our loyalty lies and to share in the upbuilding of the Kingdom of God.

(vi) There is the joy of *news of the loved one* (2: 28). Life is full of separations, and there is always joy when news comes to us of those loved ones from whom we are temporarily separated. A great Scottish preacher once spoke of the joy that man can give with a postage stamp. It is worth remembering how easily we can bring joy to those who love us and how easily we can bring anxiety, by keeping in touch or failing to keep in touch with them.

(vii) There is the joy of *Christian hospitality* (2: 29). There is the home of the shut door and there is the home of the open door. The shut door is the door of selfishness; the open door is the door of Christian welcome and Christian love. It is a great thing to have a door from which the stranger and the one in trouble know that they will never be turned away.

(viii) There is the joy of *the man in Christ* (3: 1; 4: 1). We have already seen that to be in Christ to live in his presence as the bird lives in the air, the fish in the sea, and the roots of the trees in the soil. It is human nature to be happy when we are with the person whom we love; and Christ is the lover from whom nothing in time or eternity can ever separate us.

(ix) There is the joy of *the man who has won one soul for Christ* (4: 1). The Philippians are Paul's joy and crown, for he was the means of bringing them to Jesus Christ. It is the joy of the parent, the teacher, the preacher to bring others, especially the child, into the love of Jesus Christ. Surely he who enjoys a great privilege cannot rest content until he shares it with his family and his friends. For the Christian evangelism is not a duty; it is a joy.

(x) There is the joy *in a gift* (4: 10). This joy does not lie so much in the gift itself, as in being remembered and realizing that some one cares. This is a joy that we could bring to others far oftener than we do.

THE MARKS OF THE CHRISTIAN LIFE

(ii) THE CHRISTIAN SACRIFICE

Philippians 1: 3–11 (*continued*)

IN verse 6 Paul says that he is confident that God who has begun a good work in the Philippians will complete it so that they will be ready for the day of Christ. There is a picture here in the Greek which it is not possible to reproduce in translation. The point is that the words Paul uses for *to begin* (*enarchesthai*) and for *to complete* (*epitelein*) are technical terms for the beginning and the ending of a sacrifice.

There was an initial ritual in connection with a Greek sacrifice. A torch was lit from the fire on the altar and then dipped into a bowl of water to cleanse it with its sacred flame; and with the purified water the victim and the people were sprinkled to make them holy and clean. Then followed what was known as the *euphēmia,* the sacred silence, in which the worshipper was meant to make his prayers to his god. Finally a basket of barley was brought, and some grains of the barley were scattered on the victim, and on the ground round about it. These actions were the *beginning* of the sacrifice, and the technical term for making this beginning was the verb *enarchesthai* which Paul uses here. The verb used for completing the whole ritual of sacrifice was the verb *epitelein* which Paul uses here for *to complete*. Paul's whole sentence moves in an atmosphere of sacrifice.

Paul is seeing the life of every Christian as a sacrifice ready to be offered to Jesus Christ. It is the same picture as he draws when he urges the Romans to present their bodies as a living sacrifice, holy and acceptable to God (*Romans* 12: 1).

On the day when Christ comes it will be like the coming of a king. On such a day the king's subjects are bound to present him with gifts to mark their loyalty and to show their love. The only gift Jesus Christ desires from us is ourselves. So, then, a man's supreme task is to make his life fit to offer to him. Only the grace of God can enable us to do that.

THE MARKS OF THE CHRISTIAN LIFE

(iii) THE CHRISTIAN PARTNERSHIP

Philippians 1: 3–11 (*continued*)

IN this passage the idea of *Christian partnership* is strongly stressed. There are certain things which Christians share.

(i) Christians are *partners in grace*. They are people who owe a common debt to the grace of God.

(ii) Christians are *partners in the work of the gospel*. Christians do not only share a gift; they also share a task; and that task is the furtherance of the gospel. Paul uses two words to express the work of Christians for the sake of the gospel; he speaks of the *defence* and the *confirmation* of the gospel. The defence (*apologia*) of the gospel means its defence against the attacks which come from outside. The Christian has to be ready to be a defender of the faith and to give a reason for the hope that is in him. The confirmation (*bebaiōsis*) of the gospel is the building up of its strength from within, the edifying of Christians. The Christian must further the gospel by defending it against the attacks of its enemies and by building up the faith and devotion of its friends.

(iii) Christians are *partners in suffering for the gospel*. Whenever the Christian is called upon to suffer for the sake of the gospel, he must find strength and comfort in the memory that he is one of a great fellowship in every age and every generation and every land who have suffered for Christ rather than deny their faith.

(iv) Christians are *partners with Christ*. In verse 8 Paul has a very vivid saying. The literal translation is, "I yearn for you all with the *bowels* of Jesus Christ." The Greek word for bowels is *splagchna*. The *splagchna* were the upper intestines, the heart,

the liver, and the lungs. These the Greeks believed to be the
seat of the emotions and the affections. So Paul is saying: "I
yearn for you with the very compassion of Jesus Christ himself.
I love you as Jesus loves you." The love which Paul feels
towards his Christian friends is nothing other than the love of
Christ himself. J. B. Lightfoot, writing on this passage says,
"The believer has no yearnings apart from his Lord; his pulse
beats with the pulse of Christ; his heart throbs with the heart
of Christ." When we are really one with Jesus, his love goes
out through us to our fellow-men whom he loves and for whom
he died. The Christian is a partner in the love of Christ.

THE MARKS OF THE CHRISTIAN LIFE

(iv) THE CHRISTIAN PROGRESS AND THE CHRISTIAN GOAL

Philippians 1: 3–11 (*continued*)

IT was Paul's prayer for his people that their love would grow
greater every day (verses 9 and 10). That love, which was not
merely a sentimental thing, was to grow in knowledge and in
sensitive perception so that they would be more and more able
to distinguish between right and wrong. Love is always the way
to knowledge. If we love any subject, we want to learn more
about it; if we love any person, we want to learn more about
him; if we love Jesus, we will want to learn more about him
and about his truth.

Love is always sensitive to the mind and the heart of the one
it loves. If it blindly and blunderingly hurts the feelings of the
one it claims to love, it is not love at all. If we really love
Jesus, we will be sensitive to his will and his desires; the more
we love him; the more we will instinctively shrink from what is
evil and desire what is right. The word Paul uses for *testing*
the things that differ is *dokimazein*, which is the word used for
testing metal to see that it is genuine. Real love is not blind; it will
enable us always to see the difference between the false and
the true.

So, then, the Christian will become himself pure and will cause no other to stumble. The word used for *pure* is interesting. It is *eilikrinēs*. The Greeks suggested two possible derivations, each of which has a vivid picture. It may come from *eilē, sunshine,* and *krinein,* to *judge,* and may describe that which is able to stand the test of the sunshine, without any flaw appearing. On that basis the word means that the Christian character can stand any light that is turned upon it. The other possibility is that *eilikrinēs* is derived from *eilein* which means to whirl round and round as in a sieve and so to sift until every impurity is extracted. On that basis the Christian character is cleansed of all evil until it is altogether pure.

But the Christian is not pure; he is also *aproskopos,* he never causes any other person to stumble. There are people who are themselves faultless, but who are so austere that they drive people away from Christianity. The Christian is himself pure, but his love and gentleness are such that he attracts others to the Christian way and never repels them from it.

Finally, Paul sets down the Christian aim. This is to live such a life that the glory and the praise are given to God. Christian goodness is not meant to win credit for a man himself; it is meant to win praise for God. The Christian knows, and witnesses, that he is what he is, not by his own unaided efforts, but only by the grace of God.

THE BONDS DESTROY THE BARRIERS

Philippians 1: 12–14

I want you to know, brothers, that what has happened to me has resulted rather in the advancement of the gospel, because it has been demonstrated to the whole Praetorian Guard and to all the others that my imprisonment is borne for Christ's sake and in Christ's strength; and the result is that through my bonds more of the brothers have found confidence in the Lord the more exceedingly to dare fearlessly to speak the word of God.

PAUL was a prisoner but so far from his imprisonment ending his missionary activity it actually expanded it for himself and for others. In fact, the bonds destroyed the barriers. The word Paul uses for the *advancement* of the gospel is a vivid word. It is *prokopē*; the word which is specially used for the progress of an army or an expedition. It is the noun from the verb *prokoptein,* which means *to cut down in advance*. It is the verb which is used for cutting away the trees and he undergrowth, and removing the barriers which would hinder the progress of an army. Paul's imprisonment, so far from shutting the door, opened the door to new spheres of work and activity, into which he would never otherwise have penetrated.

Paul, seeing that there was no justice for him in Palestine, had appealed to Caesar, as every Roman citizen had the right to do. In due time he had been despatched to Rome under military escort, and, when he had arrived there, he had been handed over to "the captain of the guard" and allowed to live by himself under the care of a soldier who was his guard (*Acts* 28: 16). Ultimately, although still under guard, he had been allowed to have his own hired lodging (*Acts* 28: 30), which was open to all who cared to come to see him.

In the Authorized Version we read that Paul said his bonds were manifest in all the *palace*. The word translated *palace* is *praitōrion* which can mean either a place or a body of people. When it has the meaning of a place, it has three meanings. (i) Originally it meant *a general's headquarters in camp,* the tent from which he gave his orders and directed his campaign. (ii) From that it very naturally moved on to mean a general's residence; it could, therefore, mean the Emperor's residence, that is, his palace, although examples of this usage are very rare. (iii) By another natural extension it came to mean a large house or villa, the residence of some wealthy or influential man. Here *praitōrion* cannot have any of these meanings, for it is clear that Paul stayed in his own hired lodging and it does not make sense that his hired lodging was in the Emperor's palace.

So we turn to the other meaning of *praitōrion,* a body of people. In this usage it means the *Praetorian Guard,* or very much more rarely, the barracks where the Praetorian Guard were quartered. The second of these meanings we can leave on one side, for Paul would not likely have a hired lodging in a Roman barracks.

The Praetorian Guard were the Imperial Guard of Rome. They had been instituted by Augustus and were a body of ten thousand picked troops. Agustus had kept them dispersed throughout Rome and the neighbouring towns. Tiberius had concentrated them in Rome in a specially built and fortified camp. Vitellius had increased their number to sixteen thousand. They served for twelve, and later for sixteen, years. At the close of their term they received the citizenship and a grant of more than £250. Latterly they became very nearly the Emperor's private bodyguard; and in the end they became very much a problem. They were concentrated in Rome, and there came a time when the Praetorian Guard became nothing less than king-makers; for inevitably it was their nominee who was made Emperor every time, since they could impose their will by force, if need be, upon the populace. It was to the Prefect of the Praetorian Guard, their commanding officer, that Paul was handed over when he arrived in Rome.

Paul repeatedly refers to himself as a *prisoner* or as being *in bonds*. He tells the Roman Christians that, although he had done no wrong, he was delivered a *prisoner* (*desmios*) into the hands of the Romans (*Acts* 28: 17). In *Philippians* he repeatedly speaks of his *imprisonment* (*Philippians* 1: 7, 13, 14). In *Colossians* he speaks of being in bonds for the sake of Christ, and bids the Colossians to remember his bonds (*Colossians* 4: 3, 18). In *Philemon* he calls himself a prisoner of Jesus Christ, and speaks of the bonds of the gospel (*Philemon* 9, 13). In *Ephesians* he again calls himself the prisoner for Jesus Christ (*Ephesians* 3: 1).

There are two passages in which these bonds are more closely defined. In *Acts* 28: 20 he speaks of himself as *being bound with this chain*; and he uses the same word (*halusis*) in *Ephesians* 6: 20, when he speaks of himself as *an ambassador in chains*. It is in this word *halusis* that we find our key. The *halusis* was the short length of chain by which the wrist of a prisoner was bound to the wrist of the soldier who was his guard, so that escape was impossible. The situation was this. Paul had been delivered to the captain of the Praetorian Guard, to await trial before the Emperor. He had been allowed to arrange a private lodging for himself; but night and day in that private lodging there was a soldier to guard him, a soldier to whom he was chained by his *halusis* all the time. There would, of course, be a rota of guardsmen assigned to this duty; and in the two years one by one the guardsmen of the Imperial Guard would be on duty with Paul. What a chance was there! These soldiers would hear Paul preach and talk to his friends. Is there any doubt that in the long hours Paul would open up a discussion about Jesus with the soldier to whose wrist he was chained?

His imprisonment had opened the way for preaching the gospel to the finest regiment in the Roman army. No wonder he declared that his imprisonment had actually been for the furtherance of the gospel. All the Praetorian Guard knew why Paul was in prison; many of them were touched for Christ; and the very sight of this gave to the brethren at Philippi fresh courage to preach the gospel and to witness for Christ.

Paul's bonds had removed the barriers and given him access to the flower of the Roman army, and his bonds had been the medicine of courage to the brethren at Philippi.

THE ALL-IMPORTANT PROCLAMATION

Philippians 1: 15–18

Some in their preaching of Christ are actuated by envy and strife; some by goodwill. The one preach from love, because they know that I am lying here for the defence of the gospel; the other proclaim Christ for their own partisan purposes, not with pure motives, but thinking to make my bonds gall me all the more.

What then? The only result is that in every way, whether as a cloak for other purposes, or whether in truth, Christ is proclaimed. And in this I rejoice—yes, and I will rejoice.

HERE indeed the great heart of Paul is speaking. His imprisonment has been an incentive to preaching. That incentive worked in two ways. There were those who loved him; and, when they saw him lying in prison, they redoubled their efforts to spread the gospel, so that it would lose nothing because of Paul's imprisonment. They knew that the best way to delight his heart was to see that the work did not suffer because of his unavoidable absence. But others were moved by what Paul calls *eritheia* and preached for their own partisan motives. *Eritheia* is an interesting word. Originally it simply meant *working for pay*. But the man who works solely for pay works from a low motive. He is out solely to benefit himself. The word, therefore, came to describe a careerist, out for office to magnify himself; and so it came to be connected with politics and to mean *canvassing for office*. It came to describe self-seeking and selfish ambition, which was out to advance itself and did not care to what methods it stooped to attain its ends. So there were those who preached the harder now that Paul was in prison, for his imprisonment seemed to present them with a heaven-sent opportunity to advance their own influence and prestige and lessen his.

There is a lesson for us here. Paul knew nothing of personal jealousy or of personal resentment. So long as Jesus Christ was preached, he did not care who received the credit and the prestige. He did not care what other preachers said about him, or how unfriendly they were to him, or how contemptuous they were of him, or how they tried to steal a march upon him. All that mattered was that Christ was preached. All too often we resent it when someone else gains a prominence or a credit which we do not. All too often we regard a man as an enemy because he has expressed some criticism of us or of our methods. All too often we think a man can do no good because he does not do things in our way. All too often the intellectuals have no truck with the evangelicals, and the evangelicals impugn the faith of the intellectuals. All too often those who believe in the evangelism of education have no use for the evangelism of decision, and those who practise the evangelism of decision have no use for those who feel that some other approach will have more lasting effects. Paul is the great example. He lifted the matter beyond all personalities; all that mattered was that Christ was preached.

THE HAPPY ENDING

Philippians 1: 19, 20

> For I know that this will result in my salvation, because of your prayer for me, and because of the generous help the Holy Spirit of Christ gives to me, for it is my eager expectation and my hope that I shall never on any occasion be shamed into silence, but that on every occasion, even as now, I shall speak with all boldness of speech, so that Christ will be glorified in my body, whether by my life or by my death.

IT is Paul's conviction that the situation in which he finds himself will result in his salvation. Even his imprisonment, and even the almost hostile preaching of his personal enemies, will in the end turn out to his salvation. What does he mean by *his salvation*? The word is *sōteria,* and here there are three possible meanings.

(i) It may mean *safety*, in which case Paul will be saying that he is quite sure that the matter will end in his release. But that can hardly be the meaning here, since Paul goes on to say that he cannot be sure whether he will live or die.

(ii) It may mean *his salvation in heaven*. In that case Paul would be saying that his conduct in the opportunity which this situation provides will be his witness in the day of judgment. There is a great truth here. In any situation of opportunity or challenge, a man is acting not only for time, but also for eternity. A man's reaction to every situation in time is a witness for or against him in eternity.

(iii) But *sōteria* may have a wider meaning than either of these. It can mean *health, general well-being.* Paul may well be saying that all that is happening to him in this very difficult situation is the best thing for him both in time and in eternity. "God put me in this situation; and God means it, with all its problems and its difficulties, to make for my happiness and usefulness in time, and for my joy and peace in eternity."

In this situation Paul knows that he has two great supports. (i) He has the support of the prayers of his friends. One of the loveliest things in Paul's letters is the way in which he asks again and again for his friends' prayers. "Brethren," he writes to the Thessalonians, "pray for us." "Finally, brethren," he writes, "pray for us, that the word of the Lord may speed on and triumph" (1 *Thessalonians* 5: 25; 2 *Thessalonians* 3: 1, 2). He says to the Corinthians "You must help us by prayer." (2 *Corinthians* 1: 11). He writes that he is sure that through Philemon's prayers he will be given back to his friends (*Philemon* 22). Before he sets out on his perilous journey to Jerusalem, he writes to the Church at Rome asking for their prayers (*Romans* 15: 30–32).

Paul was never too big a man to remember that he needed the prayers of his friends. He never talked to people as if he could do everything and they could do nothing; he always remembered that neither he, nor they, could do anything without the help of God. There is something to be remembered here. When people are in sorrow, one of their greatest comforts is the awareness that others are bearing them to the throne of grace. When they have to face some back-breaking effort or some heart-breaking decision, there is new strength in remembering that others are remembering them before God. When they go into new places and are far from home, it is an upholding thing to know that the prayers of those who love them are crossing continents to bring them before the throne of grace. We cannot call a man our friend unless we pray for him.

(ii) Paul knows that he has the support of the Holy Spirit. The presence of the Holy Spirit is the fulfilment of the promise of Jesus that he will be with us to the end of the world.

In all this situation Paul has one expectation and one hope.

The word he uses for *expectation* is very vivid and unusual; no one uses it before Paul and he may well have coined it himself. It is *apokaradokia*. *Apo* means *away from, kara the head, dokein to look*; and *apokaradokia* means the eager, intense look, which turns away from everything else to fix on the one object of desire. Paul's hope is that he will never be shamed into silence, either by cowardice or a feeling of ineffectiveness. Paul is certain that in Christ he will find courage never to be ashamed of the gospel; and that through Christ his labours will be made effective for all men to see. J. B. Lightfoot writes, "The right of free speech is the badge, the privilege, of the servant of Christ." To speak the truth with boldness is not only the *privilege* of the servant of Christ; it is also his *duty*.

So, then, if Paul courageously and effectively seizes his opportunity, Christ will be glorified in him. It does not matter how things go with him. If he dies, his will be the martyr's crown; if he lives, his will be the privilege still to preach and to witness for Christ. As Ellicott nobly puts it, Paul is saying, "My body will be the theatre in which Christ's glory is displayed." Here is the terrible responsibility of the Christian. Once we have chosen Christ, by our life and conduct we bring either glory or shame to him. A leader is judged by his followers; and Christ is judged by us.

IN LIFE AND IN DEATH

Philippians 1: 21-26

> For living is Christ to me, and death is gain. And yet—what if the continuance of my life in the flesh would produce more fruit for me? What I am to choose is not mine to declare. I am caught between two desires, for I have my desire to strike camp and to be with Christ, which is far better; but for your sake it is more essential for me to remain in this life. And I am confidently certain of this, that I will remain, and I will be with you and beside you all to help you along the road, and to increase the joy of your faith, so that you may have still further grounds for boasting in Christ because of me, when once again I come to visit you.

SINCE Paul was in prison awaiting trial, he had to face the fact that it was quite uncertain whether he would live or die; and to him it made no difference.

"Living," he says, in his great phrase, "is Christ to me." For Paul, Christ had been the *beginning* of life, for on that day on the Damascus road it was as if he had begun life all over again. Christ had been the *continuing* of life; there had never been a day when Paul had not lived in his presence, and in the frightening moments Christ had been there to bid him be of good cheer (*Acts* 18: 9, 10). Christ was the *end* of life, for it was towards his eternal presence that life ever led. Christ was the *inspiration* of life; he was the dynamic of life. To Paul, Christ had given the *task* of life, for it was he who had made him an apostle and sent him out as the evangelist of the Gentiles. To him Christ had given the *strength* for life, for it was Christ's all-sufficient grace that was made perfect in Paul's weakness. For him Christ was the *reward* of life, for to Paul the only worthwhile reward was closer fellowship with his Lord. If Christ were to be taken out of life, for Paul there would be nothing left.

"For me," said Paul, "death is gain". Death was entrance into Christ's nearer presence. There are passages in which Paul seems to regard death as a sleep, from which all men at some future general resurrection shall be wakened (1 *Corinthians* 16: 51, 52; 1 *Thessalonians* 4: 14, 16); but at the moment when its breath was on him Paul thought of death not as a falling asleep but as an immediate entry into the presence of his Lord. If we believe in Jesus Christ, death for us is *union* and *reunion*, union with him and reunion with those whom we have loved and lost awhile.

The result was that Paul was swayed between two desires. "I am caught," he says, "between two desires." As the Revised Standard Version has it: "I am hard pressed between the two." The word he uses is *senechomai*, the word which would be used of a traveller in a narrow defile, with a wall of rock on either hand, unable to turn aside and able only to go straight on. For himself he desired to depart and to be with Christ; for the sake of his friends and of what he could do with them and for them he desired to be left in this life. Then comes the thought that the choice is not his but God's.

"My desire is to depart," says Paul, and the phrase is very vivid. The word he uses for *to depart* is *analuein*.

(i) It is the word for striking camp, loosening the tent ropes, pulling up the tent pins and moving on. Death is a moving on. It is said that in the terrible days of the war, when the Royal Air Force stood between Britain and destruction and the lives of its pilots were being sacrificially spent, they never spoke of a pilot as having been killed but always as having been "posted to another station." Each day is a day's march nearer home, until in the end camp in this world is for ever struck and exchanged for permanent residence in the world of glory.

(ii) It is the word for loosening the mooring ropes, pulling up the anchors and setting sail. Death is a setting sail, a departure on that voyage which leads to the everlasting haven and to God.

(iii) It is the word for solving problems. Death brings life's solutions. There is some place where all earth's questions will be answered and where those who have waited will in the end understand.

It is Paul's conviction that, he will "*remain* and *continue* with them. There is a word-play in the Greek that can not be reproduced in the English. The word for to remain is *menein*; and that for to continue is *paramenein*. Lightfoot suggests the translation *bide and abide*. That keeps the word-play, but does not give the meaning. The point is this; *menein* simply means *to remain with*; but *paramenein* (*para* is the Greek for *beside*) means to wait beside a person ever ready to help. Paul's desire to live is not for his own sake, but for the sake of those whom he can continue to help.

So, then, if Paul is spared to come and see them again they will have in him grounds to boast in Jesus Christ. That is to say, they will be able to look at him and see in him a shining example of how, through Christ, a man can face the worst erect and unafraid. It is the duty of every Christian so to trust that men will be able to see what Christ can do for the man who has given his life to him.

CITIZENS OF THE KINGDOM

Philippians 1: 27–30

> One thing you must see to whatever happens—live a life that is worthy of a citizen of the Kingdom and of the gospel of Christ, so that whether I come and see you, or whether I go away and hear how things go with you, the news will be that you are standing fast, united in one spirit, fighting with one soul the battle of the gospel's faith, and that you are not put into fluttering alarm by any of your adversaries. For your steadfastness is a proof to them that they are doomed to defeat, while you are destined for salvation—and that from God. For to you has been given the privilege of doing something for Christ—the privilege of not only believing in him, but also of suffering for him, for you have the same struggle as that in which you have seen me engaged, and which now you hear that I am undergoing.

ONE thing is essential—no matter what happens either to them or to Paul the Philippians must live worthily of their faith and profession. Paul chooses his words very carefully. The Authorized Version has it: "Let your conversation be as it becometh the gospel of Christ." Nowadays this is misleading. To us *conversation* means *talk*; but it is derived from the Latin word *conversari,* which means *to conduct oneself.* In the seventeenth century a person's *conversation* was not only his way of speaking to other people; it was his whole behaviour. The phrase means: "Let your behaviour be worthy of those who are pledged to Christ."

But on this occasion Paul uses a word which he very seldom uses in order to express his meaning. The word he would normally use for to conduct oneself in the ordinary affairs of life is *peripatein,* which literally means *to walk about*;

here he uses *politeuesthai,* which means *to be a citizen.* Paul was writing from the very centre of the Roman Empire, from Rome itself; it was the fact that he was a Roman citizen that had brought him there. Philippi was a Roman colony; and Roman colonies were little bits of Rome planted throughout the world, where the citizens never forgot that they were Romans, spoke the Latin language, wore the Latin dress, called their magistrates by the Latin names, however far they might be from Rome. So what Paul is saying is, "You and I know full well the privileges and the responsibilities of being a Roman citizen. You know full well how even in Philippi, so many miles from Rome, you must still live and act as a Roman does. Well then, remember that you have an even higher duty than that. Wherever you are you must live as befits a citizen of the Kingdom of God.

What does Paul expect from them? He expects them *to stand fast.* The world is full of Christians on the retreat, who, when things grow difficult, play down their Christianity. The true Christian stands fast, unashamed in any company. He expects *unity*; they are to be bound together in one spirit like a band of brothers. Let the world quarrel; Christians must be one. He expects a certain *unconquerability.* Often evil seems invincible; but the Christian must never abandon hope or give up the struggle. He expects a *cool, calm courage.* In times of crisis others may be nervous and afraid; the Christian will be still serene, master of himself and of the situation.

If they can be like that, they will set such an example that the pagans will be disgusted with their own way of life, will realize that the Christians have something they do not possess, and will seek for very self-preservation to share it.

Paul does not suggest that this will be easy. When Christianity first came to Philippi, they saw him fight his own battle. They saw him scourged and imprisoned for the faith (*Acts* 16: 19). They know what he is now going through. But let them remember that a general chooses his best soldiers for the hardest tasks, and that it is an honour to suffer for Christ. There is a tale of a veteran French soldier who came in a desperate situation upon a young recruit trembling with fear. "Come, son," said the veteran, "and you and I will do something fine for France." So Paul says to the Philippians· "For you and for me the battle is on; let us do something fine for Christ."

THE CAUSES OF DISUNITY

Philippians 2: 1–4

If the fact that you are in Christ has any power to influence you, if love has any persuasive power to move you, if you really are sharing in the Holy Spirit, if you can feel compassion and pity, complete my joy, for my desire is that you should be in full agreement, loving the same things, joined together in soul, your minds set on the one thing. Do nothing in a spirit of selfish ambition, and in a search for empty glory, but in humility let each consider the other better than himself. Do not be always concentrating each on your own interests, but let each be equally concerned for the interests of others.

THE one danger which threatened the Philippian church was that of disunity. There is a sense in which that is the danger of every healthy church. It is when people are really in earnest and their beliefs really matter to them, that they are apt to get up against each other. The greater their enthusiasm, the greater the danger that they may collide. It is against that danger Paul wishes to safeguard his friends.

In verses 3 and 4 he gives us the three great causes of disunity.

There is *selfish ambition*. There is always the danger that people should work not to advance the work but to advance themselves. It is extraordinary how time and again the great princes of the Church almost fled from office in the agony of the sense of their own unworthiness.

Ambrose was one of the great figures of the early Church. A great scholar, he was the Roman governor of the province of Liguria and Aemilia, and he governed with such loving care that the people regarded him as a father. The bishop of the district died and the question of his successor arose. In the midst of the discussion, suddenly a little child's voice arose: "Ambrose—bishop! Ambrose—bishop!" The whole crowd took up the cry. To Ambrose it was unthinkable. He fled by night to avoid the high office the Church was offering him; and it was only the direct intervention and command of the Emperor which made him agree to become bishop of Milan.

When John Rough publicly from the pulpit in St. Andrews summoned him to the ministry, John Knox was appalled. In his own *History of the Reformation* he writes: "Thereat the said John, abashed, burst forth in most abundant tears, and withdrew himself to his chamber. His countenance and behaviour, from that day until the day that he was compelled to present himself in the public place of preaching, did sufficiently declare the grief and trouble of his heart. No man saw in him any sign of mirth, nor yet had he pleasure to accompany any man, for many days together."

Far from being filled with ambition, the great men were filled with a sense of their own inadequacy for high office.

There is the desire for *personal prestige*. Prestige is for many people an even greater temptation than wealth. To be admired and respected, to have a platform seat, to have one's opinion sought, to be known by name and appearance, even to be flattered, are for many people most desirable things. But the aim of the Christian ought to be not self-display, but self-obliteration. He should do good deeds, not that men may glorify him, but that they may glorify his Father in heaven. The Christian should desire to focus men's eyes not upon himself but on God.

There is *concentration on self*. If a man is for ever concerned first and foremost with his own interests, he is bound to collide with others. If for him life is a competition whose prizes he must win, he will always think of other human beings as enemies or at least as opponents who must be pushed out of the way. Concentration on self inevitably means elimination of others; and the object of life becomes not to help others up but to push them down.

THE CURE OF DISUNITY

Philippians 2: 1–4 (*continued*)

IN face of this danger of disunity Paul sets down five considerations which ought to prevent disharmony.

(i) The fact that we are all in Christ should keep us in unity. No man can walk in disunity with his fellow-men and in unity with Christ. If he has Christ as the companion of his way, he is inevitably the companion of every wayfarer. A man's relationships with his fellow-men are no bad indication of his relationship with Jesus Christ.

(ii) The power of Christian love should keep us in unity. Christian love is that unconquered good-will which never knows bitterness and never seeks anything but the good of others. It is not a mere reaction of the heart, as human love is; it is a victory of the will, achieved by the help of Jesus Christ. It does not mean loving only those who love us; or those whom we like; or those who are lovable. It means an unconquerable good-will even to those who hate us, to those whom we do not like, to those who are unlovely. This is the very essence of the Christian life; and it affects us in time and in eternity. Richard Tatlock in *In My Father's House* writes: "Hell is the eternal condition of those who have made relationship with God and their fellows an impossibility through lives which have destroyed love. . . . Heaven, on the other hand, is the eternal condition of those who have found real life in relationships-through-love with God and their fellows."

(iii) The fact that they share in the Holy Spirit should keep Christians from disunity. The Holy Spirit binds man to God and man to man. It is the Spirit who enables us to live that life of love, which is the life of God; if a man lives in disunity with his fellow-men, he thereby shows that the gift of the Spirit is not his.

(iv) The existence of human compassion should keep men from disunity. As Aristotle had it long ago, men were never meant to be snarling wolves but to live in fellowship together. Disunity breaks the very structure of life.

(v) Paul's last appeal is the personal one. There can be no happiness for him so long as he knows that there is disunity in the Church which is dear to him. If they would complete his joy, let them complete their fellowship. It is not with a threat that Paul speaks to the Christians of Philippi but with the appeal of love, which ought ever to be the accent of the pastor, as it was the accent of his Lord.

TRUE GODHEAD AND TRUE MANHOOD

Philippians 2: 5–11

> Have within yourselves the same disposition of mind as was in Christ Jesus, for he was by nature in the very form of God, yet he did not regard existence in equality with God as something to be snatched at, but he emptied himself, and took the very form of a slave, and became like men. And when he came in appearance as a man for all to recognise, he became obedient even to the extent of accepting death, even the death of a cross. And for that reason God exalted him, and granted to him the name which is above every name, in order that at the name of Jesus every knee should bow, of things in heaven, and things upon the earth, and things below the earth, and that every tongue should confess that Jesus Christ is Lord to the glory of God the Father.

IN many ways this is the greatest and most moving passage Paul ever wrote about Jesus. It states a favourite thought of his. The essence of it is in the simple statement Paul made to the Corinthians that, although Jesus was rich, yet for our sakes he became poor (2 *Corinthians* 8: 9). Here that simple idea is stated with a fulness which is without parallel. Paul is pleading with the Philippians to live in harmony, to lay aside their discords, to shed their personal ambitions and their pride and their desire for prominence and prestige, and to have in their hearts that humble, selfless desire to serve, which was the essence of the life of Christ. His final and unanswerable appeal is to point to the example of Jesus Christ.

This is a passage which we must try fully to understand, because it has so much in it to awaken our minds to thought and our hearts to wonder. To this end we must look closely at some of its great Greek words.

Greek is a far richer language than English. Where English has one word to express an idea, Greek has often two or three or more. In one sense these words are synonyms, but they never mean entirely the same thing; they always have some special flavour. That is particularly so of this passage. Every word is chosen by Paul with meticulous care to show two things—the reality of the manhood and the reality of the godhead of Jesus Christ. Let us take the phrases one by one. We will set them down both in the Authorized Version and in our own translation, and then try to penetrate to the essential meaning behind them.

Verse 6: *Being in the form of God*; *he was by nature in the very form of God*. Two words are most carefully chosen to show the unchangeable godhead of Jesus Christ. The word which the Authorized Version translates *being* is from the Greek verb *huparchein* which is not the common Greek word for *being*. It describes that which a man is in his very essence and which cannot be changed. It describes that part of a man which, in any circumstances, remains the same. So Paul begins by saying that Jesus was essentially and unalterably God.

He goes on to say that Jesus was in the *form* of God. There are two Greek words for *form*, *morphē* and *schēma*. They must both be translated *form,* because there is no other English equivalent, but they do not mean the same thing. *Morphē* is the essential form which never alters; *schēma* is the outward form which changes from time to time and from circumstance to circumstance. For instance, the *morphē* of any human being is humanity and this never changes; but his *schēma* is continually changing. A baby, a child, a boy, a youth, a man of middle age, an old man always have the *morphē* of humanity, but the outward *schēma* changes all the time. Roses, daffodils, tulips, chrysanthemums, primroses, dahlias, lupins all have the one *morphē* of flowers; but their *schēma* is different. Aspirin, penicillin, cascara, magnesia all have the one *morphē* of drugs; but their *schēma* is different. The *morphē* never alters; the *schēma* continually does. The word Paul uses for Jesus being in the *form* of God is *morphē*; that is to say, his unchangeable being is divine. However his outward *schēma* might alter, he remained in essence divine.

Jesus *did not think it robbery to be equal with God; he did not regard existence in equality with God as something to be snatched at*. The word used for *robbery,* which we have translated *a thing to be snatched at, is harpagmos* which comes from a verb meaning *to snatch,* or *to clutch*. The phrase can mean one of two things, both of which are at heart the same. (*a*) It can mean that Jesus did not need to snatch at equality with God, because he had it as a right. (*b*) It can mean that he did not clutch at equality with God, as if to hug it jealously to himself, but laid it willingly down for the sake of men. However we take this, it once again stresses the essential godhead of Jesus.

Verse 7: *He emptied himself; he made himself of no reputation*. The Greek is the verb *kenoun* which means literally *to empty*. It can be used of removing things from a container, until the container is empty; of pouring something out, until there is nothing left. Here Paul uses the most vivid possible word to make clear *the sacrifice of the Incarnation*. The glory of divinity Jesus gave up willingly in order to become man. He emptied himself of his deity to take upon himself his humanity. It is useless to ask how; we can only stand in awe at the sight of him, who is almighty God, hungry and weary and in tears. Here in the last reach of human language is the great saving truth that he who was rich for our sakes became poor.

He took upon him the form of a servant; he took the very

form of a slave. The word used for *form* is *morphē,* which we have seen means the essential form. Paul means that when Jesus became man it was no play-acting but reality. He was not like the Greek gods, who sometimes, so the stories ran, became men but kept their divine privileges. Jesus truly became man. *But* there is something more here. *He was made in the likeness of men*; *he became like men*. The word which the Authorized Version translates *made* and which we have translated *became* is a part of the Greek verb *gignesthai*. This verb describes *a state which is not a permanent state*. The idea is that of *becoming*, and it describes a changing phase which is completely real but which passes. That is to say, the manhood of Jesus was not permanent; it was utterly real, but it passed.

Verse 8: *He was found in fashion as a man*; *he came in appearance as a man for all to recognise*. Paul makes the same point. The word the Authorized Version has translated *fashion* and which we have translated *appearance* is *schēma,* and we have seen that this indicates a form which alters.

Verses 6–8 form a very short passage; but there is no passage in the New Testament which so movingly sets out the utter reality of the godhead and the manhood of Jesus and makes so vivid the sacrifice that he made when he laid aside his godhead and took manhood upon him. How it happened, we cannot tell, but it is the mystery of a love so great that, although we can never fully understand it, we can blessedly experience it and adore it.

HUMILIATION AND EXALTATION

Philippians 2: 5–11 (*continued*)

IT is always to be remembered that when Paul thought and spoke about Jesus, his interest and his intention were never primarily intellectual and speculative; they were always practical. To him theology and action were always bound together. Any system of thought must necessarily become a way of life. In many ways this passage is one of the greatest reaches of theological thought in the New Testament, but its aim was to persuade the Philippians to live a life in which disunity, discord, and personal ambition had no place.

So, then, Paul says of Jesus that he humbled himself and became obedient unto death, even the death of a cross. The great characteristics of Jesus's life were humility, obedience, and self-renunciation. He did not desire to dominate men but only to serve them; he did not desire his own way but only God's way; he did not desire to exalt himself but only to renounce all his glory for the sake of men. Again and again the New Testament is sure that only the man who humbles himself will be exalted (*Matthew* 23: 12; *Luke* 14: 11; 18: 14). If humility, obedience, and self-renunciation were the supreme characteristics of the life of Jesus, they must also be the hall-marks of the Christian. Selfishness, self-seeking and self-display destroy our likeness to Christ and our fellowship with each other.

But the self-renunciation of Jesus Christ brought him the greater glory. It made certain that some day, soon or late, every living creature in all the universe, in heaven, in earth and even in hell, would worship him. It is to be carefully noted whence that worship comes. *It comes from love*. Jesus won the hearts of men, not by blasting them with power, but by showing them a love they could not resist. At the sight of this person who laid his glory by for men and loved them to the extent of dying for them on a cross, men's hearts are melted and their resistance is broken down. When men worship Jesus Christ, they fall at his feet in wondering love. They do not say "I cannot resist a might like that," but, "Love so amazing, so divine, demands my life, my soul, my all." Worship is founded, not on fear, but on love.

Further, Paul says that, as a consequence of his sacrificial love, God gave Jesus the name which is above every name. One of the common biblical ideas is the giving of a new name to mark a new stage in a man's life. Abram became Abraham when he received the promise of God (*Genesis* 17: 5). Jacob became Israel when God entered into the new relationship with him (*Genesis* 32: 28). The promise of the Risen Christ to both Pergamos and to Philadelphia is the promise of a new name (*Revelation* 2: 17; 3: 12).

What then is the new name given to Jesus Christ? We cannot be quite certain what exactly was in Paul's mind, but most likely the new name is *Lord*.

The great title by which Jesus came to be known in the early Church was *kurios, Lord*, which has an illuminating history. (i) It began by meaning *master* or *owner*. (ii) It became the official title of the Roman Emperors. (iii) It became the title of the heathen gods. (iv) It was the word by which the Hebrew *Jehovah* was translated in the Greek version of the Hebrew scriptures. So, then, when Jesus was called *kurios, Lord,* it meant that he was the Master and the Owner of all life; he was the King of kings; he was the Lord in a way in which the heathen gods and the dumb idols could never be; he was nothing less than divine.

ALL FOR GOD

Philippians 2: 5–11 (*continued*)

PHILIPPIANS 2: 11 is one of the most important verses in the New Testament. In it we read that the aim of God, is a day when every tongue will confess that *Jesus Christ is Lord*. These four words were the first creed that the Christian Church ever had. To be a Christian was to confess that Jesus Christ is Lord (cp. *Romans* 10: 9). This was a simple creed, yet all-embracing. Perhaps we would do well to go back to it. Later men tried to define more closely what it meant and argued and quarrelled about it, calling each other heretics and fools. But it is still true that if man can say, "For me Jesus Christ is Lord," he is a Christian. If he can say that, he means that for him Jesus Christ is unique and that he is prepared to give him an obedience he is prepared to give no one else. He may not be able to put into words who and what he believes Jesus to be; but, so long as there is in his heart this wondering love and in his life this unquestioning obedience, he is a Christian, because Christianity consists less in the mind's understanding than it does in the heart's love.

So we come to the end of this passage; and, when we come to its end, we come back to its beginning. The day will come when men will call Jesus Lord, but they will do so *to the glory of God the Father*. The whole aim of Jesus is not his own glory but God's. Paul is clear about the lonely and ultimate supremacy of God. In the first letter to the Corinthians he writes that in the end the Son himself shall be subject to him who put all things under him (1 *Corinthians* 15: 28). Jesus draws men to himself that he may draw them to God. In the Philippian Church there were men whose aim was to gratify a selfish ambition; the aim of Jesus was to serve others, no matter what depths of self-renunciation that service might involve. In the Philippian Church there were those whose aim was to focus men's eyes upon themselves; the aim of Jesus was to focus men's eyes upon God.

So the follower of Christ must think always, not of himself but of others, not of his own glory but of the glory of God.

CO-OPERATION IN SALVATION

Philippians 2: 12–18

So then, my beloved, just as at all times you obeyed not only as in my presence, but much more, as things now are, in my absence, carry to its perfect conclusion the work of your own salvation with fear and trembling; for it is God, who, that he may carry out his own good pleasure, brings to effect in you both the initial willing and the effective action. Do all things without murmurings and questionings, that you may show yourselves blameless and pure, the spotless children of God in a warped and twisted generation, in which you appear like lights in the world, as you hold forth the word which is life, so that on the day of Christ it may be my proud claim that I have not run for nothing and that I have not toiled for nothing. But if my own life is to be poured out on the sacrifice and service of your faith, I rejoice and I do rejoice with you all. So also do you rejoice, and share my rejoicing.

PAUL'S appeal to the Philippians is more than an appeal to live in unity in a given situation; it is an appeal to live a life which will lead to the salvation of God in time and in eternity.

Nowhere in the New Testament is the work of salvation more succinctly stated. As the Revised Standard Version has it in verses 12 and 13: "Work out your own salvation with fear and trembling; for God's at work in you, both to will and to work for his good pleasure." As always with Paul, the words are meticulously chosen.

Work out your own salvation; the word he uses for *work out* is *katergazesthai,* which always has the idea of bringing to completion. It is as if Paul says: "Don't stop halfway; go on until the work of salvation is fully wrought out in you." No Christian should be satisfied with anything less than the total benefits of the gospel.

"For God is at *work* in you both to will and *to do* of his good pleasure." The word Paul uses for *work* and *do* is the same, the verb *energein.* There are two significant things about it; it is always used of *the action of God,* and it is always used of *effective action.* God's action cannot be frustrated, nor can it remain half-finished; it must be fully effective.

As we have said, this passage gives a perfect statement of the work of salvation.

(i) Salvation is of God. (*a*) It is God that works in us the desire to be saved. It is true that "our hearts are restless till they rest in him," and it is also true that "we could not even begin to seek him unless he had already found us." The desire for the salvation of God is not kindled by any human emotion but by God himself. The beginning of the process of salvation is awakened by God. (*b*) The continuance of that process is dependent on God. Without his help there can be no progress in goodness; without his help no sin can be conquered and no virtue achieved. (*c*) The end of the process of salvation is with

God, for its end is friendship with God, in which we are his and he is ours. The work of salvation is begun, continued and ended in God.

(ii) There is another side to this. Salvation is of man. "Work out your own salvation," Paul demands. Without man's co-operation, even God is helpless. The fact is that any gift or any benefit has to be received. A man may be ill and the doctor able to prescribe the drugs that will cure him; but the man will not be cured until he takes them and he may stubbornly refuse all persuasion to take them. It is so with salvation. The offer of God is there; without it there can be no such thing as salvation. But no man can ever receive salvation unless he answers God's appeal and takes what he offers.

There can be no salvation without God, but what God offers man must take. It is never God who withholds salvation; it is always man who deprives himself of it.

THE SIGNS OF SALVATION

Philippians 2: 12–18 (*continued*)

WHEN we examine the chain of thought in this passage, we see that Paul sets down five signs of salvation, as we may call them.

(i) There is the sign of *effective action*. The Christian must give continual evidence in his daily life that he is indeed working out his own salvation; day by day it must be more fully accomplished. The great tragedy of so many of us is that we are never really any further on. We continue to be victims of the same habits and slaves of the same temptations, and guilty of the same failures. But the truly Christian life must be a continual progress, for it is a journey towards God.

(ii) There is the sign of *fear and trembling*. This is not the fear and trembling of the slave cringing before his master; nor fear and trembling at the prospect of punishment. It comes from two things. It comes, first, from a sense of our own creatureliness and our own powerlessness to deal with life triumphantly. That is to say, it is not the fear and trembling which drives us to hide from God, but rather the fear and trembling which drives us to seek God, in the certainty that without his help we cannot effectively face life. It comes, second, from a horror of grieving God. When we really love a person, we are not afraid of what he may do to us; we are afraid of what we may do to him. The Christian's great fear is of crucifying Christ again.

(iii) There is the sign of *serenity and certainty*. The Christian will do all things without *murmurings and questionings*. The word which Paul uses for *murmurings* (*goggusmos*) is unusual. In the Greek of the sacred writers it has a special connection. It is the word used of the rebellious murmurings of the children of Israel in their desert journey. The people murmured against Moses (*Exodus* 15: 24; 16: 2; *Numbers* 16: 41). *Goggusmos*—pronounced *gongusomos*—is an onomatopoetic word. It describes the low, threatening, discontented muttering of a mob who distrust their leaders and are on the verge of an uprising. The word Paul uses for questionings is *dialogismos* which describes useless, and sometimes ill-natured, disputing and doubting. In the Christian life there is the serenity and the certainty of perfect certainty and perfect trust.

(iv) There is the sign of *purity*. Christians, as the Revised Standard Version has it, are to be *blameless* and *innocent* and without *blemish*. Each of these words makes its contribution to the idea of Christian purity.

(*a*) The word translated *blameless* is *amemptos* and expresses *what the Christian is to the world*. His life is of such purity that none can find anything in it with which to find fault. It is often said in courts of law that the proceedings must not only *be* just but must *be seen* to be just. The Christian must not only be pure, but the purity of his life must be seen by all.

(*b*) The word translated *innocent* is *akeraios,* and expresses *what the Christian is in himself. Akeraios* literally means *unmixed, unadulterated.* It is used, for instance, of wine or milk which is not mixed with water and of metal which has no alloy in it. When used of people, it implies motives which are unmixed. Christian purity must issue in a complete sincerity of thought and character.

(c) The word which is translated *without blemish* is *amōmos* and describes *what the Christian is in the sight of God*. This word is specially used in connection with sacrifices that are fit to be offered on the altar of God. The Christian life must be such that it can be offered like an unblemished sacrifice to God.

Christian purity is blameless in the sight of the world, sincere within itself, and fit to stand the scrutiny of God.

(v) There is the sign of *missionary endeavour*. The Christian offers to all the word of life, that is to say, the word which gives life. This Christian missionary endeavour has two aspects. (a) It is the proclamation of the offer of the gospel in words which are clear and unmistakable. (b) It is the witness of a life that is absolutely straight in a world which is warped and twisted. It is the offer of light in a world which is dark. Christians are to be *lights in the world*. The word used for *lights* (*phōstēres*) is the same as is used in the creation story of the *lights* (the sun and the moon) which God set in the firmament of the heavens to give light upon the earth (*Genesis* 1: 14–18). The Christian offers and demonstrates straightness in a twisted world and light in a dark world.

THE PICTURES OF PAUL

Philippians 2: 12–18 (*continued*)

THIS passage concludes with two vivid pictures, which are typical of Paul's way of thinking.

(i) He longs for the Christian progress of the Philippians so that at the end of the day he may have the joy of knowing that he has not run or laboured in vain. The word he uses for *to labour* is *kopian*. There are two possible pictures in it. (a) It may paint a picture of the most exacting toil. *Kopian* means to labour to the point of utter exhaustion. (*b*) It may be that *kopian* describes the toil of the athlete's training and that what Paul is saying is that he prays that all the discipline of training that he imposed upon himself may not go for nothing.

One of the features of Paul's writing is his love of pictures from the life of the athlete. And there is little wonder. In every Greek city the gymnasium was far more than a physical training-ground. It was in the gymnasium that Socrates often discussed the eternal problems; it was in the gymnasium that the philosophers and the sophists and the wandering teachers and preachers often found their audience. In any Greek city the gymnasium was not only the physical training-ground but also the intellectual club of the city. In the Greek world there were the great Isthmian Games at Corinth, the great Pan-Ionian Games at Ephesus, and, greatest of all, the Olympic Games, held every four years. The Greek cities were often at variance and frequently at war; but when the Olympic Games came round, no matter what dispute was raging, a month's truce was declared that there might be a contest in fellowship between them. Not only did the athletes come, but the historians and the poets came to give readings of their latest works, and the sculptors, whose names are immortal, came to make statues of the winners.

There can be little doubt that, in Corinth and in Ephesus, Paul had been a spectator of these games. Where there were crowds of men, Paul would be there to seek to win them for Christ. But, apart from the preaching, there was something about these athletic contests which found an answer in the heart of Paul. He knew the contests of the boxers (1 *Corinthians* 9: 26). He knew the foot-race, most famous of all the contests. He had seen the herald summoning the racers to the starting-line (1 *Corinthians* 9: 27); he had seen the runners press along the course to the goal (*Philippians* 3: 14); he had seen the judge awarding the prize at the end of the race (2 *Timothy* 4: 8); he knew of the victor's laurel crown and of his exultation (1 *Corinthians* 9: 24; *Philippians* 4: 1). He knew the rigorous discipline of training which the athlete must undertake, and the strict regulations which must be observed (1 *Timothy* 4: 7, 8; 2 *Timothy* 2: 5).

So his prayer is that he may not be like an athlete whose training and effort have gone for nothing. For him the greatest prize in life was to know that through him others had come to know and to love and to serve Jesus Christ.

(ii) But in verse 17 Paul has another picture. He had a special gift for speaking in language that people could understand. Again and again he took his pictures from the ordinary affairs of the people to whom he was speaking. He has already taken a picture from the games; now he takes one from heathen sacrifice. One of the commonest kinds of heathen sacrifice was a *libation*, which was a cup of wine poured out as an offering to the gods. For instance, every heathen meal began and ended with such a libation, as a kind of grace before and after meat. Paul here looks upon the faith and service of the Philippians as a sacrifice to God. He knows that his death may not be very far away, for he is writing in prison and awaiting trial. So he says, as the Revised Standard Version has it, that he is quite ready "to be poured as a libation upon the sacrificial offering" of their faith. In other words what he is saying to the Philippians is: "Your Christian fidelity and loyalty are already a sacrifice to God; and if death for Christ should come to me, I am willing and glad that my life should be poured out like a libation on the altar on which your sacrifice is being made."

Paul was perfectly willing to make his life a sacrifice to God; and, if that happened, to him it would be all joy, and he calls on them not to mourn at the prospect but rather to rejoice. To him every call to sacrifice and to toil was a call to his love for Christ, and therefore he met it not with regret and complaint but with joy.

THE FAITHFUL HENCHMAN

Philippians 2: 19–24

I hope in the Lord Jesus soon to send Timothy to you, that I may find out how things are going with you and take heart. I have no one with a mind equal to his, for he is the kind of man who will genuinely care for your affairs; for all men are concerned with their own interests, and not with the interests of Jesus Christ. You know his tried and tested character, and you know that, as a child serves a father, so he has shared my service in the work of the gospel. So then, I hope to send him, as soon as I see how things go with me. But I am confident in the Lord that I myself too will soon come to you.

SINCE Paul cannot himself come to Philippi, it is his intention to send Timothy as his representative. There was no one so close to him as Timothy was. We know very little detail about Timothy but the record of his service with Paul shows his fidelity.

He was a native either of Derbe or of Lystra. His mother Eunice was a Jewess and his grandmother's name was Lois. His father was a Greek and the fact that he was not circumcised would seem to show that he was educated in Greek ways (*Acts* 16: 1; 2 *Timothy* 1: 5). We cannot tell how or when he was converted to Christianity, but on his second missionary journey Paul met him and saw in him one whom he could clearly use in the service of Jesus Christ.

From that time Paul and Timothy were very close. Paul could speak of him as his child in the Lord (1 *Corinthians* 4: 17). He was with Paul in Philippi (*Acts* 16); he was with him in Thessalonica and Berea (*Acts* 17; 1–14); he was with him in Corinth and in Ephesus (*Acts* 18: 5; 19: 21, 22); and he was with him in prison in Rome (*Colossians* 1: 1; *Philippians* 1: 1). He was associated with Paul in the writing of no fewer than five of his letters—1 and 2 *Thessalonians, 2 Corinthians, Colossians* and *Philippians*; and when Paul wrote to Rome Timothy was joined with him in sending greetings (*Romans* 16: 21).

Timothy's great use was that, whenever Paul wished for information from some Church or wished to send advice or encouragement or rebuke and could not go himself, it was he whom he sent. So Timothy was sent to Thessalonica (1

Thessalonians 3: 6); to Corinth (1 *Corinthians* 4: 17; 16: 10, 11); to Philippi. In the end Timothy, too, was a prisoner for Christ's sake (*Hebrews* 13: 23).

Timothy's great value was that he was always willing to go anywhere; and in his hands a message was as safe as if Paul had delivered it himself. Others might be consumed with selfish ambition; but Timothy's one desire was to serve Paul and Jesus Christ. He is the patron saint of all those who are quite content with the second place, so long as they can serve.

THE COURTESY OF PAUL

Philippians 2: 25–30

> I think it necessary to send to you Epaphroditus, my brother, and fellow-worker, and fellow-soldier, your messenger and the servant of my need, because he is longing for you all, and he is very distressed because you heard that he had been ill, so ill that he nearly died. But God had pity on him, and not on him only, but on me too, that I might not have grief upon grief. So, then, I send him to you with the more despatch, that, when you see him, you may be glad again, and that I may be less grieved. Welcome him in the Lord with all joy, and hold such men in honour, because he came near to death because of his work for Christ, hazarding his life, that he might fill up that part of your service to me which you were personally unable to supply.

THERE is a dramatic story behind this. When the Philippians heard that Paul was in prison, their warm hearts were moved to action. They sent a gift to him by the hand of Epaphroditus. What they could not personally do, because distance prevented them, they delegated to Epaphroditus to do for them. Not only did they intend him to be the bearer of their gift; they also intended him to stay in Rome and be Paul's personal servant and attendant. Clearly Epaphroditus was a brave man, for any one who proposed to offer himself as the personal attendant of a man awaiting trial on a capital charge was laying himself open to the very considerable risk of becoming involved in the same charge. In truth, Epaphroditus risked his life to serve Paul.

In Rome Epaphroditus fell ill, perhaps with the notorious Roman fever which sometimes swept the city like a scourge, and was near to death. He knew that news of his illness had filtered back to Philippi, and he was worried because he knew that his friends there would be worried about him. God in his mercy spared the life of Epaphroditus and so spared Paul yet more sorrow. But Paul knew that it was time that Epaphroditus went back home, and in all probability he was the bearer of this letter.

But there was a problem. The Philippian Church had sent Epaphroditus to stay with Paul, and if he came back home, there would not be lacking those who said that he was a quitter. Here Paul gives him a tremendous testimonial, which will silence any possible criticism of his return.

In this testimonial every word is carefully chosen. Epaphroditus was his brother, his fellow-worker, and his fellow-soldier. As Lightfoot puts it, Epaphroditus was one with Paul in sympathy, one with him in work, one with him in danger. He in truth had stood in the firing-line. Then Paul goes on to call him your *messenger* and the *servant* of my need. It is impossible to supply the flavour of these words in translation.

The word Paul uses for messenger is *apostolos*. *Apostolos* literally means *anyone who is sent out on an errand,* but Christian usage had ennobled it and by using it Paul by implication ranks Epaphroditus with himself and all the apostles of Christ.

The word he uses for *servant* is *leitourgos*. In secular Greek this was a magnificent word. In the ancient days in the Greek cities there were men who, because they loved their city so much, at their own expense undertook certain great civic duties. It might be to defray the expenses of an embassy, or the cost of putting on one of the dramas of the great poets, or of training the athletes who would represent the city in the games, or of fitting out a warship and paying a crew to serve in the navy of the state. These men were the supreme benefactors of the state and they were known as *leitourgoi*.

Paul takes the great Christian word *apostolos* and the great

Greek word *leitourgos,* and applies them to Epaphroditus. "Give a man like that a welcome home," he says. "Hold him in honour for he hazarded his life for Christ."

Paul is making it easy for Epaphroditus to go home. There is something very wonderful here. It is touching to think of Paul, himself in the very shadow of death, in prison and awaiting judgment, showing such Christian consideration for Epaphroditus. He was facing death, and yet it mattered to him that Epaphroditus should not meet with embarrassment when he went home. Paul was a true Christian in his attitude to others; for he was never so immersed in his own troubles that he had no time to think of the troubles of his friends.

There is a word in this passage which later had a famous usage. The Authorized Version speaks of Epaphroditus *not regarding his life*; the Revised Standard Version uses *risking* his life; we have translated it *hazarding* his life. The word is the verb *paraboleuesthai*; it is a gambler's word and means to stake everything on a turn of the dice. Paul is saying that for the sake of Jesus Christ Epaphroditus gambled his life. In the days of the Early Church there was an association of men and women called the *parabolani,* the gamblers. It was their aim to visit the prisoners and the sick, especially those who were ill with dangerous and infectious diseases. In A.D. 252 plague broke out in Carthage; the heathen threw out the bodies of their dead and fled in terror. Cyprian, the Christian bishop, gathered his congregation together and set them to burying the dead and nursing the sick in that plague-stricken city; and by so doing they saved the city, at the risk of their lives, from destruction and desolation.

There should be in the Christian an almost reckless courage which makes him ready to gamble with his life to serve Christ and men.

THE INDESTRUCTIBLE JOY

Philippians 3: 1

As for what remains, my brothers, rejoice in the Lord. It is no trouble to me to write the same things to you, and for you it is safe.

PAUL sets down two very important things.

(i) He sets down what we might call the indestructibility of Christian joy. He must have felt that he had been setting a high challenge before the Philippian Church. For them there was the possibility of the same kind of persecution, and even the same kind of death, as threatened himself. From one point of view it looked as if Christianity was a grim job. But in it and beyond it all there was joy. "Your joy," said Jesus, "no one will take from you" (*John* 16: 22).

There is a certain indestructibility in Christian joy; and it is so, because Christian joy is *in the Lord*. Its basis is that the Christian lives for ever in the presence of Jesus Christ. He can lose all things, and he can lose all people, but he can never lose Christ. And, therefore, even in circumstances where joy would seem to be impossible and there seem to be nothing but pain and discomfort, Christian joy remains, because not all the threats and terrors and discomforts of life can separate the Christian from the love of God in Christ Jesus his Lord (*Romans* 8: 35–39).

In 1756 a letter came to John Wesley from a father who had a prodigal son. When the revival swept England the son was in York gaol. "It pleased God," wrote the father, "not to cut him off in his sins. He gave him time to repent; and not only so, but a heart to repent." The lad was condemned to death for his misdeeds; and the father's letter goes on: "His peace increased daily, till on Saturday, the day he was to die, he came out of the condemned-room, clothed in his shroud, and went into the cart. As he went on, the cheerfulness and composure of his countenance were amazing to all the spectators." The lad had found a joy which not even the scaffold could take away.

It often happens that men can stand the great sorrows and the great trials of life but are undone by what are almost minor inconveniences. But this Christian joy enables a man to accept even them with a smile. John Nelson was one of Wesley's most famous early preachers. He and Wesley carried out a mission in Cornwall, near Land's End, and Nelson tells about it. "All that time, Mr. Wesley and I lay on the floor: he had my greatcoat for a pillow, and I had Burkitt's notes on the New Testament for mine. After being here near three weeks, one morning about three o'clock Mr. Wesley turned over, and, finding me awake, clapped me on the side, saying: 'Brother Nelson, let us be of good cheer: I have one whole side yet, for the skin is off but on one side!' " They had little enough even to eat. One morning Wesley had preached with great effect: "As we returned, Mr. Wesley stopped his horse to pick the blackberries, saying: 'Brother Nelson, we ought to be thankful that there are plenty blackberries; for this is the best country I ever saw for getting a stomach, but the worst I ever saw for getting food!' " Christian joy made Wesley able to accept the great blows of life, and also to greet the lesser discomforts with a jest. If the Christian really walks with Christ, he walks with joy.

(ii) Here also Paul sets down what we might call the necessity of repetition. He says that he proposes to write things to them that he has written before. This is interesting, for it must mean that Paul had written other letters to the Philippians which have not survived. This is nothing to be surprised at. Paul was writing letters from A.D. 48 to A.D. 64, sixteen years, but we possess only thirteen. Unless there were long periods when he never put pen to paper there must have been many more letters which are now lost.

Like any good teacher, Paul was never afraid of repetition. It may well be that one of our faults is our desire for novelty. The great saving truths of Christianity do not change; and we cannot hear them too often. We do not tire of the foods which are the essentials of life. We expect to eat bread and to drink water every day; and we must listen again and again to the truth which is the bread and the water of life. No teacher must find it a trouble to go over and over again the great basic truths of the Christian faith; for that is the way to ensure the safety of his hearers. We may enjoy the "fancy things" at meal times, but it is the basic foods on which we live. Preaching and teaching and studying the side-issues may be attractive, and these have their place, but the fundamental truths can neither be spoken nor heard too often for the safety of our souls.

THE EVIL TEACHERS

Philippians 3: 2, 3

> Be on your guard against the dogs; be on your guard against the evil workers; be on your guard against the party of mutilation; for we are the truly circumcised, we who worship in the Spirit of God; we whose proud boast is in Jesus Christ, we who place no confidence in merely human things.

QUITE suddenly Paul's accent changes to that of warning. Wherever he taught, the Jews followed him and tried to undo his teaching. It was the teaching of Paul that we are saved by grace alone, that salvation is the free gift of God, that we can never earn it but can only humbly and adoringly accept what God has offered to us; and, further, that the offer of God is to all men of all nations and that none is excluded. It was the teaching of these Jews that, if a man wished to be saved, he must earn credit in the sight of God by countless deeds of the law; and, further that salvation belonged to the Jews and to no one else, and that, before God could have any use for him, a man must be circumcised and, as it were, become a Jew. Here Paul rounds upon these Jewish teachers who were seeking to undo his work. He calls them three things, carefully chosen to throw their claims back upon themselves.

(i) "Beware of *the dogs*," he says. With us the dog is a well-loved animal, but it was not so in the East in the time of Jesus. The dogs were the pariah dogs, roaming the streets, sometimes in packs, hunting amidst the garbage dumps and snapping and snarling at all whom they met. J. B. Lightfoot speaks of "the dogs which prowl about eastern cities, without a home and without an owner, feeding on the refuse and filth of the streets, quarrelling among themselves, and attacking the passer-by."

In the Bible the dog always stands for that than which nothing can be lower. When Saul is seeking to take his life, David's demand is: "After whom do you pursue? After a dead dog! after a flea!" (1 *Samuel* 24: 14, cp. 2 *Kings* 8: 13; *Psalm* 22: 16, 20). In the parable of the Rich Man and Lazarus, part of the torture of Lazarus is that the street dogs annoy him by licking his sores (*Luke* 16: 21). In *Deuteronomy* the Law brings together the price of a dog and the hire of a whore, and declares that neither must be offered to God (*Deuteronomy* 23: 18). In *Revelation* the word *dog* stands for those who are so impure that they are debarred from the Holy City (*Revelation* 22: 15). That which is holy must never be given to dogs (*Matthew* 7: 6). It is the same in Greek thought; the dog stands for everything that is shamelessly unclean.

It was by this name that the Jews called the Gentiles. There is a Rabbinic saying, "The nations of the world are like dogs." So this is Paul's answer to the Jewish teachers. He says to them, "In your proud self-righteousness, you call other men dogs; but it is you who are dogs, because you shamelessly pervert the gospel of Jesus Christ." He takes the very name the Jewish teachers would have applied to the impure and to the Gentiles and flings it back at themselves. A man must always have a care that he is not himself guilty of the sins of which he accuses others.

(ii) He calls them *evil workers,* workers of evil things. The Jews would be quite sure that they were workers of righteousness. It was their view that to keep the Law's countless rules and regulations was to work righteousness. But Paul was certain that the only kind of righteousness there is comes from casting oneself freely upon the grace of God. The effect of their teaching was to take men further away from God instead of to bring them nearer to him. They thought they were working good, but in fact they were working evil. Every teacher must be more anxious to listen to God than to propagate his own opinions or he, too, will run the risk of being a worker of evil, even when he thinks that he is a worker of righteousness.

THE ONLY TRUE CIRCUMCISION

Philippians 3: 2, 3 *(continued)*

(iii) Lastly, he calls them, *the party of mutilation*. There is a pun in the Greek which is not transferable to English. There are two Greek verbs which are very like each other. *Peritemnein* means *to circumcise*; *katatemnein* means *to mutilate,* as in *Leviticus* 21: 5, which describes forbidden self-mutilation, such as castration. Paul says, "You Jews think that you are circumcised; in point of fact, you are only mutilated."

What is the point of this? According to Jewish belief, circumcision was ordained upon Israel as sign and symbol that they were the people with whom God had entered into a special relationship. The story of the beginning of that sign is in *Genesïs* 17: 9, 10. When God entered into his special covenant with Abraham, circumcision was laid down as its eternal sign. Now, circumcision is only a sign in the flesh, something done to a man's body. But if a man is to be in special relationship with God, something far more is needed than a mark in his body. He must have a certain kind of mind and heart and character. This is where at least some of the Jews made the mistake. They regarded circumcision *in itself* as being enough to set them apart specially for God. Long, long before this, the great teachers and the great prophets had seen that circumcision of the flesh is by itself not nearly enough and that there was needed a spiritual circumcision. In *Leviticus* the sacred law-giver says that the *uncircumcised hearts* of Israel must be humbled to accept the punishment of God (*Leviticus* 26: 41). The summons of the writer of *Deuteronomy* is: "Circumcise the foreskin of your heart and be no longer stubborn" (*Deuteronomy* 10: 16). He says that the Lord will circumcise their hearts to make them love him (*Deuteronomy* 30: 6). Jeremiah speaks of the uncircumcised ear, the ear that will not hear the word of God (*Jeremiah* 6: 10). The writer of *Exodus* speaks of uncircumcised lips (*Exodus* 6: 12).

So what Paul says is, "If you have nothing to show but

circumcision of the flesh, you are not really circumcised—you are only mutilated. Real circumcision is devotion of heart and mind and life to God."

Therefore, says Paul, it is the Christians who are the truly circumcised. They are circumcised, not with the outward mark in the flesh, but with that inner circumcision of which the great law-givers and teachers and prophets spoke. What then are the signs of that real circumcision? Paul sets out three.

(i) We worship in the Spirit of God; or, we worship God in the Spirit. Christian worship is not a thing of ritual or of the observation of details of the Law; it is a thing of the heart. It is perfectly possible for a man to go through an elaborate liturgy and yet have a heart that is far away from God. It is perfectly possible for him to observe all the outward observances of religion and yet have hatred and bitterness and pride in his heart. The true Christian worships God, not with outward forms and observances, but with the true devotion and the real sincerity of his heart. His worship is love of God and service of men.

(ii) Our only boast is in Jesus Christ. The only boast of the Christian is not in what he has done for himself but in what Christ has done for him. His only pride is that he is a man for whom Christ died.

> In the Cross of Christ I glory,
> Towering o'er the wrecks of Time;
> All the light of sacred story
> Gathers round its head sublime.

(iii) We place no confidence in merely human things. The Jew placed his confidence in the physical badge of circumcision and in the performance of the duties of the Law. The Christian places his confidence only in the mercy of God and in the love of Jesus Christ. The Jew in essence trusted himself; the Christian in essence trusts God.

The real circumcision is not a mark in the flesh; it is that true worship, that true glory, and that true confidence in the grace of God in Jesus Christ.

THE PRIVILEGES OF PAUL

Philippians 3 : 4–7

And yet it remains true that I have every ground of confidence from the human point of view. If anyone has reason to think that he has grounds for confidence in his human heritage and attainments, I have more. I was circumcised when I was eight days old: I am of the race of Israel, of the tribe of Benjamin: I am a Hebrew, born of Hebrew parents. As far as the Law goes, I was a Pharisee: as for zeal, I was a persecutor of the Churches: as for the righteousness which is in the Law, I was beyond blame. But such things as I could humanly reckon as profits, I came to the conclusion were all loss for the sake of Jesus Christ.

PAUL has just attacked the Jewish teachers and insisted that it is the Christians, not the Jews, who are the truly circumcised and covenant people. His opponents might have attempted to say, "But you are a Christian and do not know what you are talking about; you do not know what it is to be a Jew." So Paul sets out his credentials, not in order to boast but to show that he had enjoyed every privilege which a Jew could enjoy and had risen to every attainment to which a Jew could rise. He knew what it was to be a Jew in the highest sense of the term, and had deliberately abandoned it all for the sake of Jesus Christ. Every phrase in this catalogue of Paul's privileges has its special meaning; let us look at each one.

(i) He had been *circumcised when he was eight days old.* It had been the commandment of God to Abraham: "He that is eight days old shall be circumcised among you" (*Genesis* 17: 12); and that commandment had been repeated as a permanent law of Israel (*Leviticus* 12: 3). By this claim Paul makes it clear that he is not an Ishmaelite, for the Ishmaelites were circumcised in their thirteenth year (*Genesis* 17: 25), nor a proselyte who had come late into the Jewish faith and been circumcised in manhood. He stresses the fact that he had been born into the Jewish faith and had known its privileges and observed its ceremonies since his birth.

(ii) He was of *the race of Israel.* When the Jews wished to stress their special relationship to God in its most unique sense it was the word *Israelite* that they used. *Israel* was the name which had been specially given to Jacob by God after his wrestling with him (*Genesis* 32: 28). It was to Israel that they in the most special sense traced their heritage. In point of fact the Ishmaelites could trace their descent to Abraham, for Ishmael was Abraham's son by Hagar; the Edomites could trace their descent to Isaac, for Esau, the founder of the Edomite nation, was Isaac's son; but it was the Israelites alone who could trace their descent to Jacob, whom God had called by the name of Israel. By calling himself an Israelite, Paul stressed the absolute purity of his descent.

(iii) He was *of the tribe of Benjamin*. That is to say, he was not only an Israelite; he belonged to the élite of Israel. The tribe of Benjamin had a special place in the aristocracy of Israel. Benjamin was the child of Rachel, the well-loved wife of Jacob, and of all the twelve patriarchs he alone had been born in the Promised Land (*Genesis* 35: 17, 18). It was from the tribe of Benjamin that the first king of Israel had come (1 *Samuel* 9: 1, 2), and it was no doubt .'rom that very king that Paul had been given his original name of Saul. When, under Rehoboam, the kingdom had been split up, ten of the tribes went off with Jeroboam and Benjamin was the only tribe which remained faithful with Judah (1 *Kings* 12: 21). When they returned from the exile, it was from the tribes of Benjamin and Judah that the nucleus of the reborn nation was formed (*Ezra* 4: 1). The tribe of Benjamin had the place of honour in Israel's battle-line, so that the battle-cry of Israel was: "After thee, O Benjamin!" (*Judges* 5: 14; *Hosea* 5: 8). The great feast of Purim, which was observed every year with such rejoicing, commemorated the deliverance of which the Book of Esther tells, and the central figure of that story was Mordecai, a Benjaminite. When Paul stated that he was of the tribe of Benjamin, it was a claim that he was not simply an Israelite but that he belonged to the highest aristocracy of Israel. It would be the equivalent in England of saying that he came over with the Normans or in America that he traced his descent to the Pilgrim fathers.

So, then, Paul claims that from his birth he was a God-fearing, Law-observing Jew; that his lineage was as pure as Jewish lineage could be; and that he belonged to the most aristocratic tribe of the Jews.

THE ATTAINMENTS OF PAUL

Philippians 3: 4–7 (*continued*)

So far Paul has been stating the privileges which came to him by birth; now he goes on to state his achievements in the Jewish faith.

(i) He was a *Hebrew born of Hebrew parents*. This is not the same as to say that he was a true Israelite. The point is this. The history of the Jews had dispersed them all over the world. In every town and in every city and in every country there were Jews. There were tens of thousands of them in Rome; and in Alexandria there were more than a million. They stubbornly refused to be assimilated to the nations amongst whom they lived; they retained faithfully their own religion and their own customs and their own laws. But it frequently happened that they forgot their own language. They became Greek-speaking of necessity because they lived and moved in a Greek environment. A Hebrew was a Jew who was not only of pure racial descent but who had deliberately, and often laboriously, retained the Hebrew tongue. Such a Jew would speak the language of the country in which he lived but also the Hebrew which was his ancestral language.

Paul claims not only to be a pure-blooded Jew but one who still spoke Hebrew. He had been born in the Gentile city of Tarsus, but he had come to Jerusalem to be educated at the feet of Gamaliel (*Acts* 22: 3) and was able, for instance, when the time came, to speak to the mob in Jerusalem in their own tongue (*Acts* 21: 40).

(ii) As far as the Law went, he was *a trained Pharisee*. This is a claim that Paul makes more than once (*Acts* 22: 3; 23: 6;

26: 5). There were not very many Pharisees, never more
than six thousand, but they were the spiritual athletes of
Judaism. Their very name means *The Separated Ones*. They
had separated themselves off from all common life and from
all common tasks in order to make it the one aim of their
lives to keep every smallest detail of the Law. Paul claims
that not only was he a Jew who had retained his ancestral
religion, but he had also devoted his whole life to its most
rigorous observance. No man knew better from personal
experience what Jewish religion was at its highest and most
demanding.

(iii) As far as zeal went, he had been *a persecutor of the
Church*. To a Jew zeal was the greatest quality in the religious
life. Phinehas had saved the people from the wrath of God,
and been given an everlasting priesthood, because he was
zealous for his God (*Numbers* 25: 11–13). It is the cry of the
Psalmist: "Zeal for thy house has consumed me." (*Psalm*
69: 9). A burning zeal for God was the hall-mark of Jewish
religion. Paul had been so zealous a Jew that he had tried
to wipe out the opponents of Judaism. That was a thing which
he never forgot. Again and again he speaks of it (*Acts* 22: 2–21;
26: 4–23; 1 *Corinthians* 15: 8–10; *Galatians* 1: 13). He was
never ashamed to confess his shame and to tell men that once
he had hated the Christ whom now he loved and sought to
obliterate the Church which now he served. It is Paul's
claim that he knew Judaism at its most intense and even
fanatical heat.

(iv) As for the righteousness which the Law could produce,
he was blameless. The word is *amemptos*, and J. B. Lightfoot
remarks that the verb *memphesthai*, from which it comes,
means *to blame for sins of omission*. Paul claims that there
was no demand of the Law which he did not fulfil.

So Paul states his attainments. He was so loyal a Jew
that he had never lost the Hebrew speech; he was not only
a religious Jew, he was a member of their strictest and the
most self-disciplined sect; he had had in his heart a burning
zeal for what he had thought was the cause of God;

and he had a record in Judaism in which no man could mark a fault.

All these things Paul might have claimed to set down on the credit side of the balance; but when he met Christ, he wrote them off as nothing more than bad debts. The things that he had believed to be his glories were in fact quite useless. All human achievement had to be laid aside, in order that he might accept the free grace of Christ. He had to divest himself of every human claim of honour that he might accept in complete humility the mercy of God in Jesus Christ.

So Paul proves to these Jews that he has the right to speak. He is not condemning Judaism from the outside. He had experienced it at its highest point; and he knew that it was nothing compared with the joy which Christ had given. He knew that the only way to peace was to abandon the way of human achievement and accept the way of grace.

THE WORTHLESSNESS OF THE LAW AND THE VALUE OF CHRIST

Philippians 3: 8, 9

> Yes, and I still count all things loss, because of the all-surpassing value of what it means to know Jesus Christ, my Lord. For his sake I have had to undergo a total abandonment of all things, and I count them as nothing better than filth fit for the refuse heap, that I may make Christ my own, and that it may be clear to all that I am in him, not because of any righteousness of my own, that righteousness whose source is the Law, but because of the righteousness which comes through Jesus Christ, the righteousness whose source is God and whose basis is faith.

PAUL has just said that he came to the conclusion that all his Jewish privileges and attainments were nothing but a total loss. But, it might be argued, that was a snap decision, perhaps later to be regretted and reversed. So here he says, "I came to that conclusion—and I still think so. It was not a decision made in a moment of impulse, but one by which I still stand fast."

In this passage the key-word is *righteousness. Dikaiosunē* is always difficult to translate in Paul's letters. The trouble is not that of seeing its meaning; the trouble is that of finding one English word which covers all it includes. Let us then try to see what Paul thinks about when he speaks about righteousness.

The great basic problem of life is to find fellowship with God and to be at peace and in friendship with him. The way to that fellowship is through righteousness, through the kind of life and spirit and attitude to himself which God desires. Because of that, righteousness nearly always for Paul has the meaning of *a right relationship with God.* Remembering that, we try to paraphrase this passage and to set down, not so much what Paul says, as what was in his mind.

He says, "All my life I have been trying to get into a right relationship with God. I tried to find it by strict adherence to the Jewish Law; but I found the Law and all its ways worse than useless to achieve that end. I found it no better than *skubala.*" *Skubala* has two meanings. In common language it was popularly derived from *kusi ballomena,* which means *that which is thrown to the dogs*; and in medical language it means *excrement,* (*dung,* as the Authorized Version translates it). So, then, Paul is saying, "I found the Law and all its ways of no more use than the refuse thrown on the garbage heap to help me to get into a right relationship with God. So I gave up trying to create a goodness of my own; I came to God in humble faith, as Jesus told me to do, and I found that fellowship I had sought so long."

Paul had discovered that a right relationship with God is based not on Law but on faith in Jesus Christ. It is not *achieved* by any man but *given* by God; not *won* by *works* but accepted in *trust.*

So he says, "Out of my experience I tell you that the Jewish way is wrong and futile. You will never get into a right relationship with God by your own efforts in keeping the Law.

You can get into a right relationship with God only by taking Jesus Christ at his word, and by accepting what God himself offers to you."

The basic thought of this passage is the uselessness of Law and the sufficiency of knowing Christ and accepting the offer of God's grace. The very language Paul uses to describe the Law—excrement—shows the utter disgust for the Law which his own frustrated efforts to live by it had brought him; and the joy that shines through the passage shows how triumphantly adequate he found the grace of God in Jesus Christ.

WHAT IT MEANS TO KNOW CHRIST

Philippians 3: 10, 11

> My object is to know him, and I mean by that, to know the power of his Resurrection, and the fellowship of his sufferings, while I continue to be made like him in his death, if by any chance I may attain to the resurrection of the dead.

PAUL has already spoken of the surpassing value of the knowledge of Christ. To that thought he now returns and defines more closely what he means. It is important to note the verb which he uses for *to know*. It is part of the verb *ginōskein*, which almost always indicates personal knowledge. It is not simply intellectual knowledge, the knowledge of certain facts or even principles. It is the personal experience of another person. We may see the depth of this word from a fact of Old Testament usage. The Old Testament uses *to know* of sexual intercourse. "Adam *knew* Eve his wife; and she conceived and bore Cain" (*Genesis* 4: 1). In Hebrew the verb is *yada* and in Greek it is translated by *ginōskein*. This verb indicates the most intimate knowledge of another person. It is not Paul's aim *to know about Christ*, but personally *to know him*. To know Christ means for him certain things.

(i) It means to know *the power of his Resurrection*. For Paul the Resurrection was not simply a past event in history, however amazing. It was not simply something which had happened to Jesus, however important it was for him. It was a dynamic power which operated in the life of the individual Christian. We cannot know everything that Paul meant by this phrase; but the Resurrection of Christ is the great dynamic in at least three different directions.

(*a*) It is the guarantee of the importance of this life and of this body in which we live. It was in the body that Christ rose and it is this body which he sanctifies (1 *Corinthians* 6: 13ff.).

(*b*) It is the guarantee of the life to come (*Romans* 8: 11; 1 *Corinthians* 15: 14ff.). Because he lives, we shall live also; his victory is our victory.

(*c*) It is the guarantee that in life and in death and beyond death the presence of the Risen Lord is always with us. It is the proof that his promise to be with us always to the end of the world is true.

The Resurrection of Christ is the guarantee that this life is worth living and that the physical body is sacred; it is the guarantee that death is not the end of life and that there is a world beyond; it is the guarantee that nothing in life or in death can separate us from him.

(ii) It means to know *the fellowship of his sufferings*. Again and again Paul returns to the thought that when the Christian has to suffer, he is in some strange way sharing the very suffering of Christ and is even filling up that suffering (2 *Corinthians* 1: 5; 4: 10, 11; *Galatians* 6: 17; *Colossians* 1: 24). To suffer for the faith is not a penalty, it is a privilege, for thereby we share the very work of Christ.

(iii) It means to *be so united with Christ that day by day we come more to share in his death, so that finally we share in his Resurrection*. To know Christ means that we share the way he walked; we share the Cross he bore; we share the death he died; and finally we share the life he lives for evermore.

To know Christ is not to be skilled in any theoretical or

theological knowledge; it is to know him with such intimacy that in the end we are as united with him as we are with those whom we love on earth and that, as we share their experiences, so we also share his.

PRESSING ON

Philippians 3: 12–16

> Not that I have already obtained this, or that I am already all complete but I press on to try to grasp that for which I have been grasped by Jesus Christ. Brothers, I do not count myself to have obtained; but this one thing I do—forgetting the things which are behind, and reaching out for the things which are in front, I press on towards the goal, in order that I may win the prize which God's upward calling in Christ Jesus is offering to me.
>
> Let all of you who have graduated in the school of Christ have the same attitude of mind to life. And if anyone is otherwise minded in any way, this too God will reveal to him. Only we must always walk according to that standard which we have already reached.

VITAL to the understanding of this passage is the correct interpretation of the Greek word *teleios* which occurs twice, rendered by the Revised Standard Version as *perfect* in verse 12 and as *mature* in verse 15. *Teleios* in Greek has a variety of interrelated meanings. In by far the most of them it does not signify what we might call abstract perfection but a kind of functional perfection, adequacy for some given purpose. It means *full-grown* in contradistinction to undeveloped; for example, it is used of a full-grown man as opposed to an undeveloped youth. It is used to mean *mature in mind* and therefore means *one who is qualified in a subject* as opposed to a mere learner. When it is used of offerings, it means *without blemish* and fit to offer God. When it is used of Christians, it often means *baptized persons who are full members of the Church,* as opposed to those who are still under instruction. In the days of the early Church it is quite often used to describe *martyrs*. A martyr is said to be *perfected by the sword*, and the day of his death is said to be the day of his *perfecting*. The idea is that a man's Christian maturity cannot go beyond martyrdom.

So when Paul uses the word in verse 12, he is saying that he is not by any means a complete Christian but is for ever pressing on. Then he uses two vivid pictures.

(i) He says that he is trying to grasp that for which he has been grasped by Christ. That is a wonderful thought. Paul felt that when Christ stopped him on the Damascus Road, he had a vision and a purpose for Paul; and Paul felt that all his life he was bound to press on, lest he fail Jesus and frustrate his dream. Every man is grasped by Christ for some purpose; and, therefore, every man should all his life press on so that he may grasp that purpose for which Christ grasped him.

(ii) To that end Paul says two things. He is *forgetting the things which are behind*. That is to say, he will never glory in any of his achievements or use them as an excuse for relaxation. In effect Paul is saying that the Christian must forget all that he has done and remember only what he has still to do. In the Christian life there is no room for a person who desires to rest upon his laurels. He is also *reaching out for the things which are in front*. The word he uses for *reaching out* (*epekteinomenos*) is very vivid and is used of a racer going hard for the tape. It describes him with eyes for nothing but the goal. It describes the man who is going *flat out* for the finish. So Paul says that in the Christian life we must forget every past achievement and remember only the goal which lies ahead.

There is no doubt that Paul is here speaking to the antinomians. They were those who denied that there was any law at all in the Christian life. They declared that they were within the grace of God and that, therefore, it did not matter what they did; God would forgive. No further discipline and no further effort were necessary. Paul is insisting that to the end of the day the Christian life is the life of an athlete pressing onwards to a goal which is always in front.

In verse 15 he again uses *teleios* and says that this must be the attitude of those who are *teleios*. What he means is: "Anyone who has come to be mature in the faith and knows what Christianity is must recognize the discipline and the effort and the agony of the Christian life." He may perhaps think differently, but, if he is an honest man, God will make it plain to him that he must never relax his effort or lower his standards but must press towards the goal, until the end.

As Paul saw it, the Christian is the athlete of Christ.

DWELLER ON EARTH BUT CITIZEN OF HEAVEN

Philippians 3: 17–21

Brothers, unite in imitating me, and keep your gaze on those who live, as you have seen us as an example. For there are many who behave in such a way—I have often spoken to you about them, and I do so now with tears—that they are enemies of the Cross of Christ. Their end is destruction: their god is their belly; that in which they glory is their shame. Men whose whole minds are earthbound! But our citizenship is in heaven, from which we also eagerly await the Lord Jesus Christ as Saviour, for he will refashion the body which we have in this state of our humiliation and make it like his own glorious body, by the working of that power of his whereby he is able to subject all things to himself.

FEW preachers would dare to make the appeal with which Paul begins this section. J. B. Lightfoot translates it: "Vie with each other in imitating me." Most preachers begin with the serious handicap that they have to say, not, "Do as I do," but, "Do as I say." Paul could say not only, "Listen to my words," but also, "Follow my example." It is worth noting in the passing that Bengel, one of the greatest interpreters of scripture who ever lived, translates this in a different way: "Become fellow-imitators with me in imitating Jesus Christ," but it is far more likely—as nearly all other interpreters are agreed—that Paul was able to invite his friends, not simply to listen to him, but also to imitate him.

There were in the Church at Philippi men whose conduct was an open scandal and who, by their lives, showed themselves to be the enemies of the Cross of Christ. Who they were is not certain. But it is quite certain that they lived gluttonous and immoral lives and used their so-called Christianity to justify themselves. We can only guess who they may have been.

They may have been Gnostics. The Gnostics were heretics who tried to intellectualize Christianity and make a kind of philosophy out of it. They began with the principle that from the beginning of time there had always been two realities—spirit and matter. Spirit, they said, is altogether good; and matter is altogether evil. It is because the world was created out of this flawed matter that sin and evil are in it. If then, matter is essentially evil, the body is essentially evil and will remain evil whatever you do with it. Therefore, do what you like with it; since it is evil anyhow it makes no difference what you do with it. So these Gnostics taught that gluttony and adultery and homosexuality and drunkenness were of no importance because they affect only the body which is of no importance.

There was another party of Gnostics who held a different kind of doctrine. They argued that a man could not be called complete until he had experienced everything that life had to offer, both good and bad. Therefore, they said, it was a man's duty to plumb the depths of sin just as much as to scale the heights of virtue.

Within the Church there were two sets of people to whom these accusations might apply. There were those who distorted the principle of Christian liberty. They said that in Christianity all law was gone and that the Christian had liberty to do what he liked. They turned Christian liberty into unchristian licence and gloried in giving their passions full play. There were those who distorted the Christian doctrine of grace. They said that, since grace was wide enough to cover every sin, a man could sin as he liked and not worry; it would make no difference to the all-forgiving love of God.

So the people whom Paul attacks may have been the clever Gnostics who produced specious arguments to justify their sinning or they may have been misguided Christians who twisted the loveliest things into justification for the ugliest sins.

Whoever they were, Paul reminds them of one great truth: "Our citizenship," he says, "is in heaven." Here was a picture the Philippians could understand. Philippi was a Roman colony. Here and there at strategic military centres the Romans set down their colonies. In such places the citizens were mostly soldiers who had served their time—twenty-one years—and who had been rewarded with full citizenship. The great characteristic of these colonies was that, wherever they were, they remained fragments of Rome. Roman dress was worn; Roman magistrates governed; the Latin tongue was spoken; Roman justice was administered; Roman morals were observed. Even in the ends of the earth they remained unshakeably Roman. Paul says to the Philippians, "Just as the Roman colonists never forget that they belong to Rome, you must never forget that you are citizens of heaven; and your conduct must match your citizenship."

Paul finishes with the Christian hope. The Christian awaits the coming of Christ, at which everything will be changed. Here the Authorized Version is dangerously misleading. In verse 21 it speaks about our *vile body*. In modern speech that would mean that the body is an utterly evil and horrible thing; but *vile* in sixteenth-century English still retained the meaning of its derivation from the Latin word *vilis* which in fact means nothing worse than *cheap, valueless*. As we are just now, our bodies are subject to change and decay, illness and death, the bodies of a state of humiliation compared with the glorious state of the Risen Christ; but the day will come when we will lay aside this mortal body which we now possess and become like Jesus Christ himself.

The hope of the Christian is that the day will come when his humanity will be changed into nothing less than the divinity of Christ, and when the necessary lowliness of mortality will be changed into the essential splendour of deathless life.

GREAT THINGS IN THE LORD

Philippians 4:1

> So, then, my brothers, whom I love and yearn for, my joy and crown, so stand fast in the Lord, beloved.

THROUGH this passage breathes the warmth of Paul's affection for his Philippian friends. He loves them and yearns for them. They are his joy and his crown. Those whom he had brought to Christ are his greatest joy when the shadows are closing about him. Any teacher knows what a thrill it is to point at some person who has done well and to be able to say: "That was one of my boys."

There are vivid pictures behind the word when Paul says that the Philippians are his crown. There are two words for *crown* in Greek, and they have different backgrounds. There is *diadēma*, which means *the royal crown*, the crown of kingship. And there is *stephanos*, the word used here, which itself has two backgrounds. (i) It was the crown of the victorious athlete at the Greek games. It was made of wild olive leaves, interwoven with green parsley, and bay leaves. To win that crown was the peak of the athlete's ambition. (ii) It was the crown with which guests were crowned when they sat at a banquet, at some time of great joy. It is as if Paul said that the Philippians were the crown of all his toil; it is as if he said that at the final banquet of God they were his festal crown. There is no joy in the world like bringing another soul to Jesus Christ.

Three times in the first four verses of this fourth chapter the words *in the Lord* occur. There are three great commands which Paul gives *in the Lord*.

(i) The Philippians are *to stand fast* in the Lord. Only

with Jesus Christ can a man resist the seductions of temptation and the weakness of cowardice. The word Paul uses for *stand fast* (*stēkete*) is the word which would be used for a soldier standing fast in the shock of battle, with the enemy surging down upon him. We know very well that there are some people in whose company it is easy to do the wrong thing and there are some in whose company it is easy to resist the wrong thing. Sometimes when we look back and remember some time when we took the wrong turning or fell to temptation or shamed ourselves, we say wistfully, thinking of someone whom we love: "If only he had been there, it would never have happened." Our only safety against temptation is to be *in the Lord,* always feeling his presence around us and about us.

> In vain the surge's angry shock,
> In vain the drifting sands:
> Unharmed upon the eternal Rock
> The eternal City stands.

The Church and the individual Christian can stand fast only when they stand in Christ.

(ii) Paul bids Euodia and Syntyche to *agree* in the Lord. There can be no unity unless it is in Christ. In ordinary human affairs it repeatedly happens that the most diverse people are held together because they all give allegiance to a great leader. Their loyalty to each other depends entirely on their loyalty to him. Take the leader away, and the whole group would disintegrate into isolated and often warring units. Men can never really love each other until they love Christ. The brotherhood of man is impossible without the lordship of Christ.

(iii) Paul bids the Philippians *to rejoice* in the Lord. The one thing all men need to learn about joy is that it has nothing to do with material things or with a man's outward circumstances. It is the simple fact of human experience that a man living in the lap of luxury can be wretched and a man in the depths of poverty can overflow with joy. A man upon whom life has apparently inflicted no blows at all can be gloomily or peevishly discontented and a man upon whom life has inflicted every possible blow can be serenely joyful.

In his rectorial address to the students of St. Andrews University, J. M. Barrie quoted the immortal letter which Captain Scott of the Antarctic wrote to him, when the chill breath of death was already on his expedition: "We are pegging out in a very comfortless spot. . . . We are in a desperate state—feet frozen, etc., no fuel, and a long way from food, but it would do your heart good to be in our tent, to hear our songs and our cheery conversation." The secret is this—that happiness depends not on things or on places, but always on persons. If we are with the right person, nothing else matters; and if we are not with the right person, nothing can make up for that absence. The Christian is in the Lord, the greatest of all friends; nothing can separate the Christian from his presence and so nothing can take away his joy.

HEALING THE BREACHES

Philippians 4: 2, 3

> I urge Euodia and I urge Syntyche to agree in the Lord. Yes, and I ask you too, true comrade in my work, help these women, because they toiled with me in the gospel, together with Clement, and my other fellow-labourers, whose names are in the book of life.

THIS is a passage about which we would very much like to know more. There is obvious drama behind it, heartbreak and great deeds, but of the *dramatis personae* we can only guess. First of all, there are certain problems to be settled in regard to the names. The Authorized Version speaks of *Euodias* and Syntyche. Syntyche is a woman's name, and *Euodias* would be a man's name. There was an ancient conjecture that Euodias and Syntyche were the Philippian gaoler and his

wife (*Acts* 16: 25–34): that they had become leading figures
in the Church at Philippi, and that they had quarrelled. But it
is certain that the name is not *Euodias* but *Euodia,* as indeed
the Revised Version, Moffatt, and the Revised Standard
Version all print it; and *Euodia* is a woman's name. Therefore,
Euodia and Syntyche were two women who had quarrelled.

It may well have been that they were women in whose homes
two of the house congregations of Philippi met. It is very
interesting to see women playing so leading a part in the affairs
of one of the early congregations for in Greece women
remained very much in the background. It was the aim of the
Greeks that a respectable woman should "see as little, hear as
little and ask as little as possible." A respectable woman never
appeared on the street alone; she had her own apartments in
the house and never joined the male members of the family
even for meals. Least of all had she any part in public life. But
Philippi was in Macedonia, and in Macedonia things were very
different. There women had a freedom and a place which they
had nowhere in the rest of Greece.

We can see this even in the narrative in *Acts* of Paul's work
in Macedonia. In Philippi Paul's first contact was with the
meeting for prayer by a riverside, and he spoke to the women
who resorted there (*Acts* 16: 13). Lydia was obviously a leading
figure in Philippi (*Acts* 16: 14). In Thessalonica many of the
chief women were won for Christianity, and the same
happened in Berea (*Acts* 17: 4, 12). The evidence of inscriptions
points the same way. A wife erects a tomb for herself and for
her husband out of their joint earnings, so she must have been
in business. We even find monuments erected to women by
public bodies. We know that in many of the Pauline Churches
(for example, in Corinth), women had to be content with a very
subordinate place. But it is well worth remembering, when we
are thinking of the place of women in the early Church and of
Paul's attitude to them, that in the Macedonian Churches they
clearly had a leading place.

There is another matter of doubt here. In this passage
someone is addressed who is called in the Revised Standard

Version *true yokefellow*. It is just barely possible that *yokefellow* is a proper name—*Sunzugos*. The word for true is *gnēsios*, which means genuine. And there may be a pun here. Paul may be saying: "I ask you, Sunzugos—and you are rightly named—to help." If *sunzugos* is not a proper name, no one knows who is being addressed. All kinds of suggestions have been made. It has been suggested that the yokefellow is Paul's wife, that he is the husband of Euodia or Syntyche called on to help his wife mend the quarrel, that it is Lydia, that it is Timothy, that it is Silas, that it is the minister of the Philippian Church. Maybe the best suggestion is that the reference is to Epaphroditus, the bearer of the letter, and that Paul is entrusting him not only with the letter, but also with the task of making peace at Philippi. Of the Clement named we know nothing. There was later a famous Clement who was bishop of Rome and who may have known Paul, but it was a common name.

There are two things to be noted.

(i) It is significant that when there was a quarrel at Philippi, Paul mobilized the whole resources of the Church to mend it. He thought no effort too great to maintain the peace of the Church. A quarrelling Church is no Church at all, for it is one from which Christ has been shut out. No man can be at peace with God and at variance with his fellow-men.

(ii) It is a grim thought that all we know about Euodia and Syntyche is that they were two women who had quarrelled! It makes us think. Suppose our life was to be summed up in one sentence, what would that sentence be? Clement goes down to history as the peacemaker; Euodia and Syntyche go down as the breakers of the peace. Suppose we were to go down to history with one thing known about us, what would that one thing be?

THE MARKS OF THE CHRISTIAN LIFE

Philippians 4: 4, 5

Rejoice in the Lord at all times. I will say it again—Rejoice!

Let your gracious gentleness be known to all men. The Lord is near.

PAUL sets before the Philippians two great qualities of the Christian life.

(i) The first is the quality of joy. "Rejoice . . . I will say it again—Rejoice!" It is as if having said, "Rejoice!" there flashed into his mind a picture of all that was to come. He himself was lying in prison with almost certain death awaiting him; the Philippians were setting out on the Christian way, and dark days, dangers and persecutions inevitably lay ahead. So Paul says, "I know what I'm saying. I've thought of everything that can possibly happen. And still I say it—Rejoice!" Christian joy is independent of all things on earth because it has its source in the continual presence of Christ. Two lovers are always happy when they are together, no matter where they are. The Christian can never lose his joy because he can never lose Christ.

(ii) Paul goes on, as the Authorized Version has it: "Let your moderation be known to all men." The word (*epieikeia*) translated *moderation* is one of the most untranslatable of all Greek words. The difficulty can be seen by the number of translations given of it. Wycliffe translates it *patience*; Tyndale, *softness*; Cranmer, *softness*; The Geneva Bible, *the patient mind*; the Rheims Bible, *modesty*; the Revised Version, *forbearance* (in the margin *gentleness*); Moffatt, *forbearance*; Weymouth, the *forbearing spirit*; the New English Bible, *magnanimity*. C. Kingsley Williams has: "Let all the world know that you will *meet a man half-way*."

The Greeks themselves explained this word as "justice and something better than justice." They said that *epieikeia* ought to come in when strict justice became unjust because of its generality. There may be individual instances where a perfectly just law becomes unjust or where justice is not the same thing as equity. A man has the quality of *epieikeia* if he knows when *not* to apply the strict letter of the law, when to relax justice and introduce mercy.

Let us take a simple example which meets every teacher

almost every day. Here are two students. We correct their examination papers. We apply justice and find that one has eighty per cent and the other fifty per cent. But we go a little further and find that the man who got eighty per cent has been able to do his work in ideal conditions with books, leisure and peace to study, while the man who got fifty per cent is from a poor home and has inadequate equipment, or has been ill, or has recently come through some time of sorrow or strain. In justice this man deserves fifty per cent and no more; but *epieikeia* will value his paper far higher than that.

Epieikeia is the quality of the man who knows that regulations are not the last word and knows when not to apply the letter of the law. A kirk session may sit with the book of practice and procedure on the table in front of it and take every one of its decisions in strict accordance with the law of the Church; but there are times when the Christian treatment of some situation demands that that book of practice and procedure should not be regarded as the last word.

The Christian, as Paul sees it, is the man who knows that there is something beyond justice. When the woman taken in adultery was brought before him, Jesus could have applied the letter of the Law according to which she should have been stoned to death; but he went beyond justice. As far as justice goes, there is not one of us who deserves anything other than the condemnation of God, but he goes far beyond justice. Paul lays it down that the mark of a Christian in his personal relationships with his fellow-men must be that he knows when to insist on justice and when to remember that there is something beyond justice.

Why should a man be like this? Why should he have this joy and gracious gentleness in his life? Because, says Paul, the Lord is at hand. If we remember the coming triumph of Christ, we can never lose our hope and our joy. If we remember that life is short, we will not wish to enforce the stern justice which so often divides men but will wish to deal with men in love, as we hope that God will deal with us. Justice is human, but *epieikeia* is divine.

THE PEACE OF BELIEVING PRAYER

Philippians 4: 6, 7

> Do not worry about anything; but in everything with prayer and supplication, with thanksgiving, let your requests be made known to God. And the peace of God, which surpasses all human thought, will stand sentinel over your hearts and minds in Christ Jesus.

FOR the Philippians life was bound to be a worrying thing. Even to be a human being and so to be vulnerable to all the chances and the changes of this mortal life is in itself a worrying thing; and in the Early Church, to the normal worry of the human situation there was added the worry of being a Christian which meant taking one's life in one's hands. Paul's solution is prayer. As M. R. Vincent puts it: "Peace is the fruit of believing prayer." In this passage there is in brief compass a whole philosophy of prayer.

(i) Paul stresses that we can take *everything* to God in prayer. As it has been beautifully put: "There is nothing too great for God's power; and nothing too small for his fatherly care." A child may take anything, great or small, to a parent, sure that whatever happens to him is of interest there, his little triumphs and disappointments, his passing cuts and bruises; we may in exactly the same way take anything to God, sure of his interest and concern.

(ii) We can bring our prayers, our supplications and our requests to God; we can pray for *ourselves*. We can pray for forgiveness for the *past,* for the things we need in the *present,* and for help and guidance for the *future*. We can take our own past and present and future into the presence of God. We can pray for *others*. We can commend to God's care those near and far who are within our memories and our hearts.

(iii) Paul lays it down that "*thanksgiving* must be the universal accompaniment of prayer." The Christian must feel, as it has been put, that all his life he is, "as it were, suspended between past and present blessings." Every prayer must surely include thanks for the great privilege of prayer itself. Paul insists that we must give thanks *in everything*, in sorrows and in joys alike. That implies two things. It implies *gratitude* and also *perfect submission* to the will of God. It is only when we are fully convinced that God is working all things together for good that we can really feel to him the perfect gratitude which believing prayer demands.

When we pray, we must always remember three things. We must remember *the love of God*, which ever desires only what is best for us. We must remember *the wisdom of God*, which alone knows what is best for us. We must remember *the power of God*, which alone can bring to pass that which is best for us. He who prays with a perfect trust in the love, wisdom and power of God will find God's peace.

The result of believing prayer is that the peace of God will stand like a sentinel on guard upon our hearts. The word that Paul uses (*phrourein*) is the military word for *standing on guard*. That peace of God, says Paul, as the Revised Standard Version has it, *passes all understanding*. That does not mean that the peace of God is such a mystery that man's mind cannot understand it, although that also is true. It means that the peace of God is so precious that man's mind, with all its skill and all its knowledge, can never produce it. It can never be of man's contriving; it is only of God's giving. The way to peace is in prayer to entrust ourselves and all whom we hold dear to the loving hands of God.

TRUE COUNTRIES OF THE MIND

Philippians 4: 8, 9

Finally, brothers, whatever things are true, whatever things have the dignity of holiness on them, whatever things are just, whatever things are pure, whatever things are winsome, whatever things are fair-spoken, if there are any things which men count excellence, and if there are any things which bring men praise, think of the value of these things. Practise these things which you have learned and received, and heard and seen in me, and the God of peace will be with you.

THE human mind will always set itself on something and Paul wished to be quite sure that the Philippians would set their minds on the right things. This is something of the utmost importance, because it is a law of life that, if a man thinks of something often enough, he will come to the stage when he cannot stop thinking about it. His thoughts will be quite literally in a groove out of which he cannot jerk them. It is, therefore, of the first importance that a man should set his thoughts upon the fine things and here Paul makes a list of them.

There are the things which are *true*. Many things in this world are deceptive and illusory, promising what they can never perform, offering a specious peace and happiness which they can never supply. A man should always set his thoughts on the things which will not let him down.

There are the things which are, as the Authorized Version has it, *honest*. This is an archaic use of *honest* in the sense of *honourable,* as the Revised Standard Version translates it. The Authorized Version suggests in the margin *venerable*. The Revised Version has *honourable* and suggests in the margin *reverend*. Moffatt has *worthy*.

It can be seen from all this that the Greek (*semnos*) is difficult to translate. It is the word which is characteristically used of the gods and of the temples of the gods. When used to describe a man, it describes a person who, as it has been said, moves throughout the world as if it were the temple of God. Matthew Arnold suggested the translation *nobly serious*. But the word really describes *that which has the dignity of holiness upon it*. There are things in this world which are flippant and cheap and attractive to the light-minded; but it is on the things which are serious and dignified that the Christian will set his mind.

There are the things which are *just*. The word is *dikaios,* and the Greeks defined the man who is *dikaios* as he who gives to gods and men what is their due. In other words, *dikaios* is the word of *duty faced and duty done*. There are those who set their minds on pleasure, comfort and easy ways. The Christian's thoughts are on duty to man and duty to God.

There are the things which are *pure*. The word is *hagnos* and describes what is morally undefiled. When it is used ceremonially, it describes that which has been so cleansed that it is fit to be brought into the presence of God and used in his service. This world is full of things which are sordid and shabby and soiled and smutty. Many a man gets his mind into such a state that it soils everything of which it thinks. The Christian's mind is set on the things which are pure; his thoughts are so clean that they can stand even the scrutiny of God.

There are the things which the Authorized Version and the Revised Standard call *lovely*. Moffatt translates *attractive*. *Winsome* is the best translation of all. The Greek is *prosphilēs*, and it might be paraphrased as *that which calls forth love*. There are those whose minds are so set on vengeance and punishment that they call forth bitterness and fear in others. There are those whose minds are so set on criticism and rebuke that they call forth resentment in others. The mind of the Christian is set on the lovely things—kindness, sympathy, forbearance—so he is a winsome person, whom to see is to love.

There are the things which are, as the Authorized Version has it, *of good report*. In the margin the Revised Version suggests *gracious*. Moffatt has *high-toned*. The Revised Standard Version has *gracious*. C. Kingsley Williams has *whatever has a good name*. It is not easy to get at the meaning of this word (*eophema*). It literally means *fair-speaking*, but it was specially connected with the holy silence at the beginning of a sacrifice in the presence of the gods. It might not be going too far to say that it describes *the things which are fit for God to hear*. There are far too many ugly words and false words and impure words in this world. On the lips and in the mind of the Christian there should be only words which are fit for God to hear.

Paul goes on, *if there be any virtue*. Both Moffatt and the Revised Standard Version use *excellence* instead of *virtue*. The word is *aretē*. The odd fact is that, although *aretē* was one of the great classical words, Paul usually seems deliberately to avoid it and this is the only time it occurs in his writings. In classical thought it described every kind of excellence. It could describe the excellence of the ground in a field, the excellence of a tool for its purpose, the physical excellence of an animal, the excellence of the courage of a soldier, and the virtue of a man. Lightfoot suggests that with this word Paul calls in as an ally all that was excellent in the pagan background of his friends. It is as if he were saying, "If the old pagan idea of excellence, in which you were brought up, has any influence over you—think of that. Think of your past life at its very highest, to spur you on to the new heights of the Christian way." The world has its impurities and its degradations but it has also its nobilities and its chivalries, and it is of the high things that the Christian must think.

Finally Paul says, *if there be any praise*. In one sense it is true that the Christian never thinks of the praise of men, but in another sense it is true that every good man is uplifted by the praise of good men. So Paul says that the Christian will live in such a way that he will neither conceitedly desire nor foolishly despise the praise of men.

THE TRUE TEACHING AND THE TRUE GOD

Philippians 4: 8, 9 (*continued*)

IN this passage Paul lays down the way of true teaching.

He speaks of the things which the Philippians have *learned*. These are the things in which he personally instructed them. This stands for the personal interpretation of the gospel which Paul brought to them. He speaks of the things which the Philippians have *received*. The word is *paralambanein* which characteristically means to accept a fixed tradition. This then stands for the accepted teaching of the Church which Paul had handed on to them.

From these two words we learn that teaching consists of two things. It consists of handing on to men the accepted body of truth and doctrine which the whole Church holds; and it consists of illuminating that body of doctrine by the personal interpretation and instruction of the teacher. If we would teach or preach we must know the accepted body of the Church's doctrine; and then we must pass it through our own minds and hand it on to others, both in its own simplicity and in the significances which our own experiences and our own thinking have given to it.

Paul goes further than that. He tells the Philippians to copy what they have heard and seen in himself. Tragically few teachers and preachers can speak like that; and yet it remains true that personal example is an essential part of teaching. The teacher must demonstrate in action the truth which he expresses in words.

Finally, Paul tells his Philippian friends that, if they faithfully do all this, the God of peace will be with them. It is of great interest to study Paul's titles for God.

(i) He is *the God of peace*. This, in fact, is his favourite title for God (*Romans* 16: 20; 1 *Corinthians* 14: 33; 1 *Thessalonians* 5: 23). To a Jew peace was never merely a negative thing, never merely the absence of trouble. It was everything which makes for a man's highest good. Only in the friendship of God can a man find life as it was meant to be. But also to a Jew this peace issued specially in *right relationships*. It is only by the grace of God that we can enter into a right relationship with him and with our fellow-men. The God of peace is able to make life what it was meant to be by enabling us to enter into fellowship with himself and with our fellow-men.

(ii) He is the *God of hope* (*Romans* 15: 13). Belief in God is the only thing which can keep a man from the ultimate despair. Only the sense of the grace of God can keep him from despairing about himself; and only the sense of the over-ruling providence of God can keep him from despairing about the world. The Psalmist sang: "Why are you cast down,

O my soul? . . . Hope in God: for I shall again praise him, my help and my God" (*Psalm* 42: 11; 43: 5). F. W. Faber wrote:

> For right is right, since God is God,
>   And right the day must win;
> To doubt would be disloyalty,
>   To falter would be sin.

The hope of the Christian is indestructible because it is founded on the eternal God.

(iii) He is *the God of patience, of comfort, and of consolation* (*Romans* 15: 5; 2 *Corinthians* 1: 3). Here we have two great words. Patience is in Greek *hupomonē*, which never means simply the ability to sit down and bear things but the ability to rise up and conquer them. God is he who gives us the power to use any experience to lend greatness and glory to life. God is he in whom we learn to use joy and sorrow, success and failure, achievement and disappointment alike, to enrich and to ennoble life, to make us more useful to others and to bring us nearer to himself. *Consolation* and *comfort* are the same Greek word *paraklēsis*. *Paraklēsis* is far more than soothing sympathy; it is encouragement. It is the help which not only puts an arm round a man but sends him out to face the world; it not only wipes away the tears but enables him to face the world with steady eyes. *Paraklēsis* is comfort and strength combined. God is he in whom any situation becomes our glory and in whom a man finds strength to go on gallantly when life has fallen in.

(iv) He is *the God of love and peace* (2 *Corinthians* 13: 11). Here we are at the heart of the matter. Behind everything is that love of God which will never let us go, which bears with all our sinning, which will never cast us off, which never sentimentally weakens but always manfully strengthens a man for the battle of life.

Peace, hope, patience, comfort, love—these were the things which Paul found in God. Indeed "our sufficiency is from God" (2 *Corinthians* 3: 5).

THE SECRET OF TRUE CONTENT

Philippians 4: 10–13

> I rejoiced greatly in the Lord that now at length you have made
> your thoughtfulness for me to blossom again. That was a matter
> indeed about which you were always thoughtful, but you had no
> opportunity. Not that I speak as if I were in a state of want, for
> I have learned to be content in whatever situation I am. I know
> both how to live in the humblest circumstances, and how to
> have far more than enough. In everything and in all things I have
> learned the secret of being well fed and of being hungry, of
> having more than enough and of having less than enough. I can
> do all things through him who infuses strength into me.

As the letter draws to an end Paul generously expresses
his gratitude for the gift which the Philippians had sent
to him. He knew that he had always been much in their
thoughts, but circumstances had up till now given them no
opportunity to show their mindfulness of him.

It was not that he was dissatisfied with his own state,
for he had learned the gift of *content*. Paul uses one of the
great words of pagan ethics (*autarkēs*), which means *entirely
self-sufficient*. *Autarkeia,* self-sufficiency, was the highest
aim of Stoic ethics; by it the Stoics meant a state of mind
in which a man was absolutely independent of all things
and of all people. They proposed to reach that state by a
certain pathway of the mind.

(i) They proposed to eliminate all desire. The Stoics rightly
believed that contentment did not consist in possessing much
but in wanting little, "If you want to make a man happy,"
they said, "add not to his possessions, but take away from his
desires." Socrates was once asked who was the wealthiest
man. He answered: "He who is content with least, for
autarkeia is nature's wealth." The Stoics believed that the
only way to content was to abolish all desire until a man had
come to a stage when nothing and no one were essential to
him.

(ii) They proposed to eliminate all emotion until a man had

come to a stage when he did not care what happened either to himself or to anyone else. Epictetus says. "Begin with a cup or a household utensil; if it breaks, say, 'I don't care.' Go on to a horse or pet dog; if anything happens to it, say, 'I don't care.' Go on to yourself, and if you are hurt or injured in any way, say, 'I don't care.' If you go on long enough, and if you try hard enough, you will come to a stage when you can watch your nearest and dearest suffer and die, and say, 'I don't care.'" The Stoic aim was to abolish every feeling of the human heart.

(iii) This was to be done by a deliberate act of will which saw in everything the will of God. The Stoic believed that literally nothing could happen which was not the will of God. However painful it might be, however disastrous it might seem, it was God's will. It was, therefore, useless to struggle against it; a man must steel himself into accepting everything.

In order to achieve content, the Stoics abolished all desires and eliminated all emotions. Love was rooted out of life and caring was forbidden. As T. R. Glover said, "The Stoics made of the heart a desert, and called it a peace."

We see at once the difference between the Stoics and Paul. The Stoic said, "I will learn content by a deliberate act of my own will." Paul said, "I can do all things through Christ who infuses his strength into me." For the Stoic contentment was a human achievement; for Paul it was a divine gift. The Stoic was *self-sufficient*; but Paul was *God-sufficient*. Stoicism failed because it was inhuman; Christianity succeeded because it was rooted in the divine. Paul could face anything, because in every situation he had Christ; the man who walks with Christ can cope with anything.

THE VALUE OF THE GIFT

Philippians 4: 14–20

All the same, I am most grateful to you for your readiness to share the burden of my troubles. You too, know, Philippians, that in the beginning of the gospel, when I left Macedonia, no Church entered into partnership with me in the matter of giving and receiving except you alone, for in Thessalonica not merely once but twice you sent to help my need. It is not that I am looking for the gift; but I am looking for the fruit which increases to your credit. I have enough and more than enough of everything. I am fully supplied, now that I have received from Epaphroditus the gifts which came from you, the odour of a sweet savour, an acceptable sacrifice, well-pleasing to God. And my God will gloriously supply every need of yours according to his wealth in Jesus Christ. Glory be to our God and Father for ever and ever. Amen.

THE generosity of the Philippian Church to Paul went back a long way. In *Acts* 16 and 17 we read how he preached the gospel in Philippi and then moved on to Thessalonica and Berea. As far back as that, the Philippian Church had given practical proof of its love for him. He was in a unique position in regard to the Philippians; from no other Church had he ever accepted any gift or help. It was in fact that very circumstance which annoyed the Corinthians (2 *Corinthians* 11: 7–12).

Paul says a fine thing. He says, "It is not that I desire a present from you for my own sake, although your gift touches my heart and makes me very glad. I don't need anything, for I have more than enough. But I am glad that you gave me a gift for your own sake, for your kindness will stand greatly to your credit in the sight of God." Their generosity made him glad, not for his own sake but for theirs. Then he uses words which turn the gift of the Philippians into a sacrifice to God. "The odour of a sweet savour," he calls it. That was a regular Old Testament phrase for a sacrifice which was acceptable to God. It is as if the smell of the sacrifice was sweet in the nostrils of God (*Genesis* 8: 21; *Leviticus* 1: 9, 13, 17). Paul's joy in the gift is not in what it did for him, but in what it did for them. It was not that he did not value the gift for its own sake; but his greatest joy was that it and the love which prompted it were dear to God.

In a last sentence, Paul lays it down that no gift ever made any man the poorer. The wealth of God is open to those who love him and love their fellow-men. He who gives makes himself richer, for his own gift opens to him the gifts of God.

GREETINGS

Philippians 4: 21–23

Greet in Christ Jesus every one of God's dedicated people. The brothers who are with me send you their greetings, especially those of Caesar's household. The grace of the Lord Jesus Christ be with your spirit.

THE letter comes to the end with greetings. In this final section there is one intensely interesting phrase. Paul sends special greetings from the Christian brothers who are of *Caesar's household*. It is important to understand this phrase rightly. It does not mean those who are of Caesar's kith and kin. Caesar's household was the regular phrase for what we would call the Imperial Civil Service; it had members all over the world. The palace officials, the secretaries, the people who had charge of the imperial revenues, those who were responsible for the day-to-day administration of the empire, all these were Caesar's household. It is of the greatest interest to note that even as early as this Christianity had penetrated into the very centre of the Roman government. There is hardly any sentence which shows more how Christianity had infiltrated even into the highest positions in the empire. It was to be another three hundred years before Christianity became the religion of the empire, but already the first signs of the ultimate triumph of Christ were to be seen. The crucified Galilaean carpenter had already begun to rule those who ruled the greatest empire in the world.

And so the letter ends: "The grace of the Lord Jesus Christ be with your spirit." The Philippians had sent their gifts to Paul. He had only one gift to send to them—his blessing. But what greater gift can we give to any man than to remember him in our prayers?

THE LETTER TO THE COLOSSIANS

INTRODUCTION TO THE LETTER TO
THE COLOSSIANS

THE TOWNS OF THE LYCUS VALLEY

About one hundred miles from Ephesus, in the valley of the River Lycus, near where it joins the Maeander, there once stood three important cities—Laodicaea, Hierapolis and Colosse. Originally they had been Phrygian cities but now they were part of the Roman province of Asia. They stood almost within sight of each other. Hierapolis and Laodicaea stood on either side of the valley with the River Lycus flowing between, only six miles apart and in full view of each other; Colosse straddled the river twelve miles farther up.

The Lycus Valley had two remarkable characteristics.

(i) It was notorious for earthquakes. Strabo describes it by the curious adjective *euseistos,* which in English means *good for earthquakes.* More than once Laodicaea had been destroyed by an earthquake, but she was a city so rich and so independent that she had risen from the ruins without the financial help which the Roman government had offered. As the John who wrote the *Revelation* was to say of her, in her own eyes she was rich and had need of nothing (*Revelation* 3: 17).

(ii) The waters of the River Lycus and of its tributaries were impregnated with chalk. This chalk gathered and all over the countryside built up the most amazing natural formations. Lightfoot writes in description of that area: "Ancient monuments are buried; fertile land is overlaid; rivers beds choked up and streams diverted; fantastic grottoes and cascades and archways of stone are formed, by this strange, capricious power, at once destructive and creative, working silently throughout the ages. Fatal to vegetation, these incrustations spread like a stony shroud over the ground. Gleaming like glaciers on the hillside, they attract the eye of the traveller at a distance of twenty miles, and form a singularly striking feature in scenery of more than common beauty and impressiveness."

A WEALTHY AREA

In spite of these things this was a wealthy area and famous for two closely allied trades. Volcanic ground is always fertile; and what was not covered by the chalky incrustations was magnificent pasture land. On these pastures there were great flocks of sheep and the area was perhaps the greatest centre of the woollen industry in the world. Laodicaea was specially famous for the production of garments of the finest quality. The allied trade was dyeing. There was some quality in those chalky waters which made them specially suitable for dyeing cloth, and Colosse was so famous for this trade that a certain dye was called by its name.

So, then, these three cities stood in a district of considerable geographical interest and of great commercial prosperity.

THE UNIMPORTANT CITY

Originally the three cities had been of equal importance, but, as the years went on, their ways parted. Laodicaea became the political centre of the district and the financial headquarters of the whole area, a city of splendid prosperity. Hierapolis became a great trade-centre and a notable spa. In that volcanic area there were many chasms in the ground from which came hot vapours and springs, famous for their medicinal quality; and people came in their thousands to Hierapolis to bathe and to drink the waters.

Colosse at one time was as great as the other two. Behind her rose the Cadmus range of mountains and she commanded the roads to the mountain passes. Both Xerxes and Cyrus had halted there with their invading armies, and Herodotus had called her "a great city of Phrygia." But for some reason the glory departed. How great that departure was can be seen from the fact that Hierapolis and Laodicaea are both to this day clearly discernible because the ruins of some great buildings still stand; but there is not a stone to show where Colosse stood and her site can only be guessed at. Even when Paul wrote Colosse was a small town; and Lightfoot says that she was the most unimportant town to which Paul ever wrote a letter.

The fact remains that in this town of Colosse there had arisen a heresy which, if it had been allowed to develop unchecked, might well have been the ruination of the Christian faith.

THE JEWS IN PHRYGIA

One other fact must be added to complete the picture. These three cities stood in an area in which there were many Jews. Many years before, Antiochus the Great had transported two thousand Jewish families from Babylon and Mesopotamia into the regions of Lydia and Phrygia. These Jews had prospered and, as always happens in such a case, more of their fellow-countrymen had come into the area to share their prosperity. So many came that the stricter Jews of Palestine lamented the number of Jews who left the rigours of their ancestral land for "the wines and baths of Phrygia."

The number of Jews who resided there can be seen from the following historical incident. Laodicaea, as we have seen, was the administrative centre of the district. In the year 62 B.C., Flaccus was the Roman governor resident there. He sought to put a stop to the practice of the Jews of sending money out of the province to pay the Temple tax. He did so by placing an embargo on the export of currency; and in his own part of the province alone he seized as contraband no less than twenty pounds of gold which was meant for the Temple at Jerusalem. That amount of gold would represent the Temple tax of no fewer than 11,000 people. Since women and children were exempt from the tax and since many Jews would successfully evade the capture of their money, we may well put the Jewish population as high as almost 50,000.

THE CHURCH AT COLOSSE

The Christian Church at Colosse was one which Paul had not himself founded and which he had never visited. He classes the Colossians and the Laodicaeans with those who had never seen his face in the flesh (2: 1). But no doubt the founding of the Church sprang from his directing. During his three years in Ephesus the whole province of Asia was evangelized, so that all its inhabitants, both Jews and Greeks, heard the word of the

Lord (*Acts* 19:10). Colosse was about one hundred miles from Ephesus and it was no doubt in that campaign of expansion that the Colossian Church was founded. We do not know who its founder was; but it may well have been Epaphras, who is described as Paul's fellow-servant and the faithful minister of the Colossian Church and who is later connected also with Hierapolis and Laodicaea (1:7; 4:12, 13). If Epaphras was not the founder of the Christian Church there, he was certainly the minister in charge of the area.

A GENTILE CHURCH

It is clear that the Colossian Church was mainly Gentile. The phrase *estranged and hostile in mind* (1:21) is the kind of phrase which Paul regularly uses of those who had once been strangers to the covenant of promise. In 1:27 he speaks of making known the mystery of Christ among the Gentiles, when the reference is clearly to the Colossians themselves. In 3:5–7 he gives a list of their sins before they became Christians, and these are characteristically Gentile sins. We may confidently conclude that the membership of the Church at Colosse was largely composed of Gentiles.

THE THREAT TO THE CHURCH

It must have been Epaphras who brought to Paul, in prison in Rome, news of the situation which was developing in Colosse. Much of the news that he brought was good. Paul is grateful for news of their faith in Christ and their love of the saints (1:4). He rejoices at the Christian fruit which they are producing (1:6). Epaphras has brought him news of their love in the Spirit (1:8). He is glad when he hears of their order and steadfastness in the faith (2:5). There was trouble at Colosse certainly; but it had not yet become an epidemic. Paul believed that prevention was better than cure; and in this letter he is grasping this evil before it has time to spread.

THE HERESY AT COLOSSE

What the heresy was which was threatening the life of the

Church at Colosse no one can tell for sure. "The Colossian Heresy" is one of the great problems of New Testament scholarship. All we can do is to go to the letter itself, list the characteristics we find indicated there and then see if we can find any general heretical tendency to fit the list.

(i) It was clearly a heresy which attacked the total adequacy and the unique supremacy of Christ. No Pauline letter has such a lofty view of Jesus Christ or such insistence on his completeness and finality. Jesus Christ is the image of the invisible God; in him all fullness dwells (1: 15, 19). In him are hid all the treasures of wisdom and of knowledge (2: 2). In him dwells the fullness of the Godhead in bodily form (2: 9).

(ii) Paul goes out of his way to stress the part that Christ played in creation. By him all things were created (1: 16); in him all things cohere (1: 17). The Son was the Father's instrument in the creation of the universe.

(iii) At the same time he goes out of his way to stress the real humanity of Christ. It was in the body of his flesh that he did his redeeming work (1: 22). The fullness of the Godhead dwells in him *sōmatikōs,* in bodily form (2: 9). For all his deity Jesus Christ was truly human flesh and blood.

(iv) There seems to have been an astrological element in this heresy. In 2: 8, as the Authorized Version has it, he says that they were walking after the *rudiments* of this world, and in 2: 20 that they ought to be dead to the *rudiments* of this world. The word translated *rudiments* is *stoicheia,* which has two meanings.

(*a*) Its basic meaning is *a row of things*; it can, for instance, be used for a file of soldiers. But one of its commonest meanings is the A B C, the letters of the alphabet, set out, as it were, in a row. From that it develops the meaning of *the elements of any subject,* the rudiments. It is in that sense that the Authorized Version takes it; and, if that is the correct sense, Paul means that the Colossians are slipping back to an elementary kind of Christianity when they ought to be going on to maturity.

(*b*) We think that the second meaning is more likely.

Stoicheia can mean *the elemental spirits of the world,* and especially the spirits of the stars and planets. The ancient world was dominated by thought of the influence of the stars; and even the greatest and the wisest men would not act without consulting them. It believed that all things were in the grip of an iron fatalism settled by the stars; and the science of astrology professed to provide men with the secret knowledge which would rid them of their slavery to the elemental spirits. It is most likely that the Colossian false teachers were teaching that it needed something more than Jesus Christ to rid men of their subjection to these elemental spirits.

(v) This heresy made much of the powers of demonic spirits. There are frequent references to *principalities* or *authorities,* which are Paul's names for these spirits (1: 16; 2: 10; 2: 15). The ancient world believed implicitly in demonic powers. The air was full of them. Every natural force—the wind, the thunder, the lightning, the rain—had its demonic super-intendent. Every place, every tree, every river, every lake had its spirit. They were in one sense intermediaries to God and in another sense barriers to him, for the vast majority of them were hostile to men. The ancient world lived in a demon-haunted universe. The Colossian false teachers were clearly saying that something more than Jesus Christ was needed to defeat the power of the demons.

(vi) There was clearly what we might call a philosophical element in this heresy. The heretics are out to spoil men with philosophy and empty deceit (2: 8). Clearly the Colossian heretics were saying that the simplicities of the gospel needed a far more elaborate and recondite knowledge added to them.

(vii) There was a tendency in this heresy to insist on the observance of special days and rituals—festivals, new moons and sabbaths (2: 16).

(viii) Clearly there was a would-be ascetic element in this heresy. It laid down laws about food and drink (2: 16). Its slogans were: "Touch not; taste not; handle not" (2: 21). It was a heresy which was out to limit Christian freedom by insistence on all kinds of legalistic ordinances.

(ix) Equally this heresy had at least sometimes an anti-nomian streak in it. It tended to make men careless of the chastity which the Christian should have and to make him think lightly of the bodily sins (3: 5–8).

(x) Apparently this heresy gave at least some place to the worship of angels (2: 18). Beside the demons it introduced angelic intermediaries between man and God.

(xi) Lastly, there seems to have been in this heresy something which can only be called spiritual and intellectual snobbery. In 1: 28 Paul lays down his aim; it is to warn *every man*; to teach *every man* in *all* wisdom; and to present *every man mature* in Jesus Christ. We see how the phrase *every man* is reiterated and how the aim is to make him *mature* in *all* wisdom. The clear implication is that the heretics limited the gospel to some chosen few and introduced a spiritual and intellectual aris-tocracy into the wide welcome of the Christian faith.

THE GNOSTIC HERESY

Was there then any general heretical tendency of thought which would include all this? There was what was called *Gnosticism*. Gnosticism began with two basic assumptions about matter. First, it believed that spirit alone was good and that matter was essentially evil. Second, it believed that matter was eternal; and that the universe was not created out of nothing—which is orthodox belief—but out of this flawed matter. Now this basic belief had certain inevitable consequences.

(i) It had an effect on the doctrine of creation. If God was spirit, then he was altogether good and could not possibly work with this evil matter. Therefore God was *not* the creator of the world. He put out a series of emanations, each of which was a little more distant from God until at the end of the series there was an emanation so distant that it could handle matter; and it was this emanation which created the world. The Gnostics went further. Since each emanation was more distant from God, it was also more ignorant of him. As the series went on that ignorance turned to hostility. So the emanations most distant from God were at once ignorant of him and hostile to him. It followed that he who created the world was at once completely ignorant of, and utterly hostile to, the true God. It was to meet that Gnostic doctrine of creation that Paul insisted that the agent of God in creation was not some ignorant and hostile power, but the Son who perfectly knew and loved the Father.

(ii) It had its effect on the doctrine of the person of Jesus Christ. If matter was altogether evil and if Jesus was the Son of God, then Jesus could not have had a flesh and blood body—so the Gnostic argued. He must have been a kind of spiritual phantom. So the Gnostic romances say that when Jesus walked, he left no footprints on the ground. This, of course, completely removed Jesus from humanity and made it impossible for him to be the Saviour of men. It was to meet this Gnostic doctrine that Paul insisted on the flesh and blood body of Jesus and insisted that Jesus saved men in the body of his flesh.

(iii) It had its effect on the ethical approach to life. If matter was evil, then it followed that our bodies were evil. If our bodies were evil, one of two consequences followed. (a) We must starve and beat and deny the body; we must practise a rigid asceticism in which the body was kept under, and in which its every need and desire were refused. (b) It was possible to take precisely the opposite point of view. If the body was evil, it did not matter what a man did with it; spirit was all that mattered. Therefore a man could sate the body's desires and it would make no difference.

Gnosticism could, therefore, issue in asceticism, with all kinds of laws and restrictions; or, it could issue in anti-nomianism, in which any immorality was justified. And we can see precisely both these tendencies at work in the false teachers at Colosse.

(iv) One thing followed from all this—Gnosticism was a highly intellectual way of life and thought. There was this long series of emanations between a man and God; man must fight his way up a long ladder to get to God. In order to do that he would need all kinds of secret knowledge and esoteric learning and hidden passwords. If he was to practise a rigid asceticism, he would need to know the rules; and so rigid would his asceticism be that it would be impossible for him to embark on the ordinary activities of life. The Gnostics were, therefore, quite clear that the higher reaches of religion were open only to the chosen few. This conviction of the necessity of belonging to an intellectual religious aristocracy precisely suits the situation at Colosse.

(v) There remains one thing to fit into this picture. It is quite obvious that there was a Jewish element in the false teaching threatening the Church at Colosse. The festivals and the new moons and the sabbaths were characteristically Jewish; the laws about food and drink were essentially Jewish levitical laws. Where then did the Jews come in? It is a strange thing that many Jews were sympathetic to Gnosticism. They knew all about angels and demons and spirits. But, above all, they said, "We know quite well that it takes special knowledge to reach God. We know quite well that Jesus and his gospel are far too simple—and that special knowledge is to be found nowhere else than in the Jewish law. It is our ritual and ceremonial law which is indeed the special knowledge which enables a man to reach God." The result was that there was not infrequently a strange alliance between Gnosticism and Judaism; and it is just such an alliance that we find in Colosse, where, as we have seen, there were many Jews.

It is clear that the false teachers of Colosse were tinged with Gnostic heresy. They were trying to turn Christianity into a philosophy and a theosophy, and, if they had been successful, the Christian faith would have been destroyed.

THE AUTHORSHIP OF THE LETTER

One question remains. Many scholars do not believe that Paul wrote this letter at all. They have three reasons.

(i) They say that in *Colossians* there are many words and phrases which do not appear in any other of Paul's letters. That is perfectly true. But it does not prove anything. We cannot demand that a man should always write in the same way and with the same vocabulary. In *Colossians* we may well believe that Paul had new things to say and found new ways to say them.

(ii) They say that the development of Gnostic thought was, in fact, much later than the time of Paul so that, if the Colossian heresy was connected with Gnosticism, the letter is necessarily later than Paul. It is true that the great written Gnostic systems are later. But the idea of two worlds and the idea of the evil of matter are deeply woven into both Jewish and Greek thought. There is nothing in *Colossians* which cannot be explained by long-standing Gnostic tendencies in ancient thought, although it is true that the systematization of Gnosticism came later.

(iii) They say that the view of Christ in *Colossians* is far in advance of any of the letters certainly written by Paul. There are two answers to that.

First, Paul speaks of the unsearchable riches of Christ. In Colosse a new situation met him and out of these unsearchable riches he drew new answers to meet it. It is true that the Christology of *Colossians* is an advance on anything in the earlier letters of Paul; but that is far from saying that Paul did not write it, unless we are willing to argue that his thought remained for ever static. It is true to say that a man thinks out the implications of his faith only as circumstances compel him to do so; and in face of a new set of circumstances Paul thought out new implications of Christ.

Second, the germ of all Paul's thought about Christ in *Colossians* does, in fact, exist in one of his earlier letters. In 1 *Corinthians* 8: 6 he writes of *one Lord Jesus Christ through whom are all things and through whom we exist*. In that phrase is the essence of all he says in *Colossians*. The seed was there in his mind, ready to blossom when a new climate and new circumstances called it into growth.

We need not hesitate to accept *Colossians* as a letter written by Paul.

THE GREAT LETTER

It remains a strange and wonderful fact that Paul wrote the

letter which contains the highest reach of his thought to so unimportant a town as Colosse then was. But in doing so he checked a tendency, which, had it been allowed to develop, would have wrecked Asian Christianity and might well have done irreparable damage to the faith of the whole Church.

COLOSSIANS

CHRISTIAN GREETINGS

Colossians 1: 1

This is a letter from Paul, an apostle of Jesus Christ by the will of God, and from Timothy, the brother, to the dedicated people of God and faithful brothers in Christ who are in Colosse.

A DEDICATED Christian cannot write a single sentence without making clear the great beliefs which underlie all his thought. Paul had never actually been in Colosse and so he has to begin by making clear what right he has to send a letter to the Colossians. He does that in one word; he is an *apostle*. The word *apostolos* literally means *one who is sent out*. Paul's right to speak is that he has been sent out by God to be his ambassador to the Gentiles. Morever, he is an apostle *by the will of God*. That office is not something which he has earned or achieved; it is something which has been given him by God. "You did not choose me," said Jesus, "but I chose you" (*John* 15: 16). Here, right at the outset of the letter, is the whole doctrine of grace. A man is not what he has made himself, but what God has made him.

With himself Paul associates Timothy; and he gives him a lovely title. He calls him *the brother,* a title which is given to Quartus (*Romans* 16: 23); to Sosthenes (1 *Corinthians* 1: 1); to Apollos (1 *Corinthians* 16: 12). The fundamental necessity for Christian service and for Christian office is *brotherliness*.

Premanand, highborn Indian who became a Christian, tells in his autobiography of Father E. F. Brown of the Oxford Mission in Calcutta. E. F. Brown was every man's friend; but he was specially the friend of the hackney carriage drivers, the carters, the tram conductors, the menial servants, and the hundreds of poor street boys. Later in his life, when he was travelling about India, Premanand would often meet people who had stayed in Calcutta, and they would always ask for E. F. Brown, saying, "Is that friend of the Calcutta street boys still alive, who used to walk arm-in-arm with the poor?" Sir Henry Lunn tells how his father used to describe his grandfather: "He was a friend of the poor without patronage, and of the rich without subservience."

To use our modern idiom, the first necessity for Christian service is the ability to "get alongside" all kinds of people. Timothy is not described as the preacher, the teacher, the theologian, the administrator, but as the *brother*. He who walks in aloofness can never be a real servant of Jesus Christ.

Another interesting and significant fact is that this opening address is to God's dedicated people and to the faithful brothers in Colosse. In the matter of opening addresses Paul's custom changed. In his earlier letters he always addressed the letter to the *Church*. 1 *and* 2 *Thessalonians*, 1 *and* 2 *Corinthians* and *Galatians* are all addressed to the *Church* of the district to which they are sent. But beginning with *Romans* his letters are all addressed to God's dedicated people in such and such a place. It is so in *Romans, Colossians, Philippians* and *Ephesians*. As Paul grew older, he came more and more to see what matters is individual people. The Church is not a kind of abstract entity; it is individual men and women and children. As the years went on, Paul began to see the Church in terms of individuals hence this style of greeting.

The opening greeting closes with a most significant placing of two things side by side. He writes to the Christians who are *in Colosse* and who are *in Christ*. A Christian always moves in two spheres. He is in a certain place in this world; but he is also in Christ. He lives in two dimensions. He lives in this world whose duties he does not treat lightly; but above and beyond that he lives in Christ. In this world he may move from place to place; but wherever he is, he is in Christ. That is why outward circumstances make little difference to the Christian; his peace and his joy are not dependent on them. That is why he will do any job with all his heart. It may be menial, unpleasant, painful, it may be far less distinguished than he might expect to have; its rewards may be small and its praise non-existent; nevertheless the

Christian will do it diligently, uncomplainingly and cheerfully, for he is in Christ and does all things as to the Lord. We are all in our own Colosse, but we are all in Christ, and it is Christ who sets the tone of our living.

THE DOUBLE COMMITMENT

Colossians 1: 2–8

> Grace be to you and peace from God our Father. We always thank God, the Father of our Lord Jesus Christ, for you in our prayers; for we have heard of your faith in Christ Jesus, and of the love you have to all God's dedicated people, because of the hope which is laid up for you in heaven. Of that hope you have already heard in the true word of the gospel, which has come to you, just as in all the world it is bearing fruit and increasing, just as it did among you too, from that day on which you heard and knew the grace of God as it truly is, as you learned it from Epaphras, my beloved fellow-bondman, who is a faithful servant of Christ on our behalf, and who has made known to us your love in the Spirit.

HERE we are presented with the essence of the Christian life. The fact which delights Paul's heart and for which he gives God thanks is that he has been told that the Colossians are showing two great qualities in their lives, *faith in Christ* and *love for their fellow-men*.

These are the two sides of the Christian life. The Christian must have faith; he must know what he believes. But he must also have love for men; he must turn that belief into action. It is not enough simply to have faith, for there can be an orthodoxy which knows no love. It is not enough only to have love for men, for without real belief that love can become mere sentimentality. The Christian has a double commitment—he is committed to Jesus Christ and he is committed to his fellow-men. Faith in Christ and love to men are the twin pillars of the Christian life.

That faith and love depend on the hope that is laid up in heaven. What exactly does Paul mean? Is he asking the

Colossians to show faith in Christ and love for men only for the hope of some reward that is going to come to them some day? Is this "pie in the sky"? There is something much deeper than that here.

Think of it this way. Loyalty to Christ may involve a man in all kinds of loss and pain and suffering. There may be many things to which he has to say goodbye. The way of love may seem to many to be the way of a fool. Why spend life in selfless service? Why not use it "to get on" as the world counts getting on? Why not push the weaker brother out of the way? The answer is—*because of the hope that is set before us.*

As C. F. D. Moule puts it, that hope is the certainty that, in spite of the world's ways, God's way of love has the last word. As James Russell Lowell put it in "The Present Crisis," the hope is that:

> Though the cause of Evil prosper, yet 'tis truth alone is strong . . .
> Truth for ever on the scaffold, Wrong for ever on the throne,—
> Yet that scaffold sways the future, and, behind the dim unknown,
> Standeth God within the shadow, keeping watch above his own.

The Christian hope is that God's way is the best way and that the only real peace, the only real joy, the only true and lasting reward are to be found in it. Loyalty to Christ may bring trouble here—but that is not the last word. The world may laugh contemptuously at the folly of the way of love— but the foolishness of God is wiser than the wisdom of man. The Christian hope is the confidence that it is better to stake one's life on God than to believe the world.

THE ESSENCE OF THE GOSPEL

Colossians 1: 2–8 (*continued*)

VERSES 6–8 are a kind of summary of what the gospel is and does. Paul has much to say of the hope, to which the Colossians have already listened and which they have already accepted.

(i) The gospel is *good news of God*. Its message is of a God who is a Friend and Lover of the souls of men. First and foremost, the gospel sets us in a right relationship with God.

(ii) The gospel is *truth*. All previous religions could be entitled "guesses about God." The Christian gospel gives a man not guesses but certainties about God.

(iii) The gospel is *universal*. It is for all the world. It is not confined to any one race or nation, nor to any one class or condition. Very few things in this world are open to all men. A man's mental calibre decides the studies he can undertake. A man's social class decides the circle amidst which he will move. A man's material wealth determines the possessions he can amass. A man's particular gifts decide the things he can do. But the message of the gospel is open without exception to all men.

(iv) The gospel is *productive*. It bears fruit and increases. It is the plain fact of history and experience that the gospel has power to change individual men and the society in which men live. It can change the sinner into a good man and can slowly take the selfishness and the cruelty out of society so that all men may have the chance God would wish them to have.

(v) The gospel tells of *grace*. It is not so much the message of what God demands as of what he offers. It tells not so much of his demand from men as of his gift to men.

(vi) The gospel is *humanly transmitted*. It was Epaphras who brought it to the Colossians. There must be a human channel through which the gospel can come to men. And this is where we come in. The possession of the good news of the gospel involves the obligation to share it. That which is divinely given must be humanly passed on. Jesus Christ needs us to be the hands and feet and lips which will bring his gospel to those who have never heard it.

THE ESSENCE OF PRAYER'S REQUEST

Colossians 1 : 9–11

That, in fact, is why, from the day we heard about it, we do not cease to pray for you, asking that you may be filled with an ever-growing knowledge of his will, in all spiritual wisdom and understanding, so that you may conduct yourselves worthily of the Lord, and in such a way as to be altogether pleasing to him, bearing fruit in every good work, and increasing in the fuller knowledge of God. May you continue to be strengthened with all strength according to his glorious power, so that you may possess all fortitude and patience with joy.

IT is a very precious thing to hear the prayers of a saint for his friends; and that is what we hear in this passage. It may well be said that this passage teaches us more about the essence of prayer's request than almost any other in the New Testament. From it we learn, as C. F. D. Moule has said, that prayer makes two great requests. It asks for the discernment of God's will and then for the power to perform that will.

(i) Prayer begins by asking that we may be filled with an ever-growing knowledge of the will of God. Its great object is to know the will of God. We are trying not so much to make God listen to us as to make ourselves listen to him; we are trying not to persuade God to do what we want, but to find out what he wants us to do. It so often happens that in prayer we are really saying, "Thy will be changed," when we ought to be saying, "Thy will be done." The first object of prayer is not so much to speak to God as to listen to him.

(ii) This knowledge of God must be translated into our human situation. We pray for spiritual wisdom and understanding. *Spiritual wisdom* is *sophia*, which we could describe as *knowledge of first principles. Understanding* is *sunesis,* which is what the Greeks sometimes described as *critical knowledge*, meaning *the ability to apply first principles to any given situation which may arise in life*. So when Paul prays that his friends may have *wisdom* and *understanding,* he is praying that they may understand the great truths of Christianity and may be able to apply them to the tasks and decisions which meet them in everyday living. A man may quite easily be a master of theology and a failure in living;

able to write and talk about the eternal truths and yet helpless to apply them to the things which meet him every day. The Christian must know what Christianity means, not in a vacuum but in the business of living.

(iii) This knowledge of God's will, and this wisdom and understanding, must issue in right conduct. Paul prays that his friends may conduct themselves in such a way as to please God. There is nothing in this world so practical as prayer. It is not escape from reality. Prayer and action go hand in hand. We pray not in order to escape life but in order to be better able to meet it.

(iv) To do this we need power. Therefore, Paul prays that his friends may be strengthened with the power of God. The great problem in life is not to know what to do but to do it. For the most part, we are well aware in any given situation what we ought to do; our problem is to put that knowledge into action. What we need is power; and that we receive in prayer. If God merely told us what his will was, that might well be a frustrating situation; but he not only tells us his will, he also enables us to perform it.

> Knowledge we ask not, knowledge thou hast lent,
> But Lord—the will, there lies our deepest need.
> Grant us to build above the high intent—
> The deed—the deed.

Through prayer we reach the greatest gift in all the world— knowledge plus power.

THE THREE GREAT GIFTS

Colossians 1: 9–11 (*continued*)

WHAT we might call the *asking* part of Paul's prayer ends with a prayer for three great qualities. He prays that his Colossian friends may possess all *fortitude, patience* and *joy*.

. *Fortitude* and *patience* are two great Greek words which often keep company. *Fortitude* is *hupomonē* and *patience* is *makrothumia.* There is a distinction between these two words. It would not be true to say that Greek always rigidly observes this distinction, but it is there when the words occur together.

Hupomonē is translated *patience* in the Authorized Version. But it does not mean patience in the sense of simply bowing the head and letting the tide of events flow over one. It means not only the ability to bear things, but the ability, in bearing them, to turn them into glory. It is a conquering patience. *Hupomonē* is the ability to deal triumphantly with anything that life can do to us.

Makrothumia is usually translated *long-suffering* in the Authorized Version. Its basic meaning is *patience with people.* It is the quality of mind and heart which enables a man so to bear with people that their unpleasantness and maliciousness and cruelty will never drive him to bitterness, that their unteachableness will never drive him to despair, that their folly will never drive him to irritation, and that their unloveliness will never alter his love. *Makrothumia* is the spirit which never loses patience with, belief in, and hope for men.

So Paul prays for *hupomonē,* the *fortitude* which no situation can defeat, and *makrothumia,* the *patience* which no person can defeat. He prays that the Christian may be such that no circumstances will defeat his strength and no human being defeat his love. The Christian's fortitude in events and patience with people must be indestructible.

Added to all this there is *joy.* The Christian way is not a grim struggle with events and with people; it is a radiant and sunny-hearted attitude to life. The Christian joy is joy in any circumstances. As C. F. D. Moule puts it: "If joy is not rooted in the soil of suffering, it is shallow." It is easy to be joyful when things go well, but the Christian radiance is something which not all the shadows of life can quench.

So the Christian prayer is: "Make me, O Lord, victorious over every circumstance; make me patient with every person; and withal give me the joy which no circumstance and no man will ever take from me."

PRAYER'S GREAT THANKSGIVING

Colossians 1: 12–14

> May you give thanks to the Father, who enabled us to obtain
> our share of the inheritance of God's dedicated people in the
> Kingdom of light; for he rescued us from the power of darkness,
> and brought us over into the kingdom of his beloved Son, in
> whom we have redemption and the forgiveness of sins.

PAUL turns to grateful thanksgiving for the benefits which the
Christian has received in Christ. There are two key ideas here.

(i) God has given to the Colossians a share in the inheritance
of God's dedicated people. There is in this whole passage a
very close correspondence with Paul's words in *Acts* when
he told Agrippa that the work God had given him was:
"To open their eyes, that they may turn from darkness to
light, and from the power of Satan to God, that they may
receive forgiveness of sins, and a place among those who
are sanctified by faith in God" (*Acts* 26: 18). The first
privilege is that there has been given to the Gentiles a share
in the inheritance of the chosen people of God. The Jews
had always been God's chosen people, but now the door
has been opened to all men.

(ii) The second key idea lies in the phrase which says, as the
Revised Standard Version has it, that God has *transferred
us to the kingdom of his beloved Son,* or, as we have translated
it, that God has *brought us over* into the kingdom of his
beloved son. The word which Paul uses for *to transfer* or
to bring over is the Greek verb *methistēmi*. This is a word
with a special use. In the ancient world, when one empire
won a victory over another, it was the custom to take the
population of the defeated country and transfer it lock, stock
and barrel to the conqueror's land. Thus the people of the
northern kingdom were taken away to Assyria, and the
people of the southern kingdom were taken away to Babylon.
So Paul says that God has transferred the Christian to his
own kingdom. That was not only a transference but a
rescue; and it meant four great things.

(*a*) It meant a transference *from darkness to light*. Without God men grope and stumble as if walking in the dark. They know not what to do; they know not where they are going. Life is lived in the shadows of doubt and in the darkness of ignorance. When Bilney the martyr read that Jesus Christ came into the world to save sinners, he said that it was like the dawn breaking on a dark night. In Jesus Christ, God has given us a light by which to live and by which to die.

(*b*) It meant a transference *from slavery to freedom*. It was *redemption,* and that was the word used for the emancipation of a slave and for the buying back of something which was in the power of someone else. Without God men are slaves to their fears, to their sins and slaves to their own helplessness. In Jesus Christ there is liberation.

(*c*) It meant a transference from *condemnation to forgiveness*. Man in his sin deserves nothing but the condemnation of God; but through the work of Jesus Christ he discovers God's love and forgiveness. He knows now that he is no longer a condemned criminal at God's judgment seat, but a lost son for whom the way home is always open.

(*d*) It meant a transference from *the power of Satan to the power of God*. Through Jesus Christ man is liberated from the grip of Satan and is able to become a citizen of the Kingdom of God. Just as an earthly conqueror transferred the citizens of the land he had conquered to a new land, so God in his triumphant love transfers men from the realm of sin and darkness into the realm of holiness and light.

THE TOTAL ADEQUACY OF JESUS CHRIST

Colossians 1: 15–23

He is the image of the invisible God, begotten before all creation, because by him all things were created, in heaven and upon earth, the things which are visible and the things which are invisible, whether thrones or lordships or powers or authorities. All things were created through him and for him. He is before all things, and in him all things cohere. He is the head of the body, that is, of the Church. He is the beginning, the firstborn from the dead, that he might be supreme in all things. For in him God in all his fullness was pleased to take up his abode, and through him to reconcile all things to himself, when he had made peace through the blood of his Cross. This was done for all things, whether on the earth or in the heavens. And you, who were once estranged and hostile in your minds, in the midst of evil deeds, he has now reconciled in the body of his flesh, through his death, in order to present you before him consecrated, unblemished, irreproachable, if only you remain grounded and stablished in the faith, not shifting from the hope of the gospel which you have heard, which has been proclaimed to every creature under heaven, of which I, Paul, have been made a servant.

THIS is a passage of such difficulty and of such importance that we shall have to spend considerable time on it. We shall divide what we must say about it into certain sections and we begin with the situation which gave it birth and with the whole view of Christ which Paul sets out in the letter.

I. THE MISTAKEN THINKERS

Colossians 1: 15–23 (*continued*)

IT is one of the facts of the human mind that a man thinks only as much as he has to. It is not until a man finds his faith opposed and attacked that he really begins to think out its implications. It is not until the Church is confronted with some dangerous heresy that she begins to realize the riches of orthodoxy. It is characteristic of Christianity that it can always produce new riches to meet a new situation.

When Paul wrote *Colossians,* he was not writing in a vacuum. He was writing, as we have already seen in the introduction, to meet a very definite situation. There was a tendency of thought in the early Church called Gnosticism. Its devotees were called *Gnostics,* which more or less means *the intellectual ones.* These men were dissatisfied with what they considered the rude simplicity of Christianity and wished to turn it into a philosophy and to align it with the other philosophies which held the field at that time.

The Gnostics began with the basic assumption that matter was altogether evil and spirit altogether good. They further held that matter was eternal and that it was out of this evil matter that the world was created. The Christian, to use the technical phrase, believes in creation out of nothing; the Gnostic believed in creation out of evil matter.

Now God was spirit and if spirit was altogether good and matter essentially evil, it followed, as the Gnostic saw it, that the true God could not touch matter and, therefore, could not himself be the agent of creation. So the Gnostics believed that God put forth a series of emanations, each a little further away from God until at last there was one so distant from God, that it could handle matter and create the world.

The Gnostics went further. As the emanations went further and further from God, they became more and more ignorant of him. And in the very distant emanations there was not only ignorance of God, but also hostility to him. The Gnostics came to the conclusion that the emanation who created the world was both ignorant of and hostile to the true God; and sometimes they identified that emanation with the God of the Old Testament.

This has certain logical consequences.

(i) As the Gnostics saw it, the creator was not God but someone hostile to him; and the world was not God's world but that of a power hostile to him. That is why Paul insists that God did create the world, and that his agent in creation was no ignorant and hostile emanation but Jesus Christ, his Son (*Colossians* 1: 16).

(ii) As the Gnostics saw it, Jesus Christ was by no means unique. We have seen how they postulated a whole series of emanations between the world and God. They insisted that Jesus was merely one of these emanations. He might stand high in the series; he might even stand highest; but he was only one of many. Paul meets this by insisting that in Jesus Christ all fullness dwells (*Colossians* 1: 19); that in him there is the fullness of the godhead in bodily form (*Colossians* 2: 9). One of the supreme objects of *Colossians* is to insist that Jesus is utterly unique and that in him there is the whole of God.

(iii) As the Gnostics saw it, this had another consequence with regard to Jesus. If matter was altogether evil, it followed that the body was altogether evil. It followed further that he who was the revelation of God, could not have had a real body. He could have been nothing more than a spiritual phantom in bodily form. The Gnostics completely denied the real manhood of Jesus. In their own writings they, for instance, set it down that when Jesus walked, he left no footprints on the ground. That is why Paul uses such startling phraseology in *Colossians*. He speaks of Jesus reconciling man to God *in his body of flesh* (*Colossians* 1: 22); he says that the fullness of the godhead dwelt in him *bodily*. In opposition to the Gnostics, Paul insisted on the flesh and blood manhood of Jesus.

(iv) The task of man is to find his way to God. As the Gnostics saw it, that way was barred. Between this world and God there was this vast series of emanations. Before the soul could rise to God, it had to get past the barrier of each of these emanations. To pass each barrier special knowledge and special passwords were needed; it was these passwords and that knowledge that the Gnostics claimed to give. This meant two things.

(*a*) It meant that salvation was *intellectual knowledge*. To meet that Paul insists that salvation is not knowledge; it is *redemption* and the *forgiveness of sins*. The Gnostic teachers held that the so-called simple truths of the gospel were not nearly enough. To find its way to God the soul needed far more than that; it needed the elaborate knowledge and the secret passwords which Gnosticism alone could give. So Paul insists that nothing more is needed than the saving truths of the gospel of Jesus Christ.

(*b*) If salvation depended on this elaborate knowledge, it was clearly not for every man but only for the intellectual. So the Gnostics divided mankind into the spiritual and the earthly; and only the spiritual could be truly saved. Full salvation was beyond the scope of the ordinary man. It is with that in mind that Paul wrote the great verse *Colossians* 1: 28. It was his aim to warn *every man* and to teach *every man,* and so to present *every man* mature in Christ Jesus. Against a salvation possible for only a limited intellectual minority, Paul presents a gospel which is for every man, however simple and unlettered or however wise and learned he may be.

These, then, were the great Gnostic doctrines; and all the time we are studying this passage, and indeed the whole letter, we must have them in our mind, for only against them does Paul's language become intelligible and relevant.

II. WHAT JESUS CHRIST IS IN HIMSELF

Colossians 1: 15–23 (*continued*)

IN this passage Paul says two great things about Jesus, both of which are in answer to the Gnostics. The Gnostics had said that Jesus was merely one among many intermediaries and that, however great he might be, he was only a partial revelation of God.

(i) Paul says that Jesus Christ is *the image* of the invisible God (*Colossians* 1: 15). Here he uses a word and a picture which would waken all kinds of memories in the minds of those who heard it. The word is *eikōn,* and *image* is its correct translation. Now, as Lightfoot points out, an image can be two things which merge into each other. It can be a *representation*; but a representation, if it is perfect enough, can become a *manifestation.* When Paul uses this word, he lays it down that Jesus is the perfect manifestation of God. To see what God is like, we must look at Jesus. He perfectly represents God to men in a form which they can see and know and understand. But it is what is behind this word that is of entrancing interest.

(*a*) The Old Testament and the inter-testamental books have a great deal to say about *Wisdom*. In *Proverbs* the great passages on Wisdom are in chapters 2 and 8. There Wisdom is said to be co-eternal with God and to have been with God when he created the world. Now in the *Wisdom of Solomon* 7: 26, *eikōn* is used of Wisdom; Wisdom is the *image* of the goodness of God. It is as if Paul turned to the Jews and said, "All your lives you have been thinking and dreaming and writing about this divine Wisdom, which is as old as God, which made the world and which gives wisdom to men. In Jesus Christ this Wisdom has come to men in bodily form for all to see." Jesus is the fulfilment of the dreams of Jewish thought.

(*b*) The Greeks were haunted by the thought of the *Logos,* the word, the reason of God. It was that Logos which created the world, which put sense into the universe, which kept the stars in their courses, which made this a dependable world, which put a thinking mind into man. This very word *eikōn* is used again and again by Philo of the Logos of God. "He calls the invisible and divine Logos, which only the mind can perceive, the *image* (*eikōn*) of God" (*Philo: Concerning the Creator of the World*: 8). It is as if Paul said to the Greeks: "For the last six hundred years you have dreamed and thought and written about the reason, the mind, the word, the Logos of God; you called it God's *eikōn*; in Jesus Christ that Logos has come plain for all to see. Your dreams and philosophies are all come true in him."

(*c*) In these connections of the word *eikōn* we have been moving in the highest realms of thought, where only the philosophers can move familiarly. But there are two much simpler connections which would immediately flash across the minds of those who heard or read this for the first time. Their minds would at once go back to the creation story. There the old story tells of the culminating act of creation. "God said, Let us make man in our *image.* . . . So God created man in his own *image,* in the *image* of God he created him" (*Genesis* 1: 26, 27). Here indeed is illumination. Man was made that he might be nothing less than the *eikōn* of God, for the word in the *Genesis* story is the same. That is what man was meant to be, but sin came in and man never achieved his destiny. By using this word of Jesus, Paul in effect says, "Look at this Jesus. He shows you not only what God is; he also shows you *what man was meant to be*. Here is manhood as God designed it. Jesus is the perfect manifestation of God and the perfect manifestation of man." There is in Jesus Christ the revelation of godhead and the revelation of manhood.

(*d*) But we come at last to something much simpler than any of these things. And there is no doubt that many of the simpler of Paul's readers would think of this. Even if they knew nothing of the Wisdom Literature and nothing of Philo and nothing of the *Genesis* story they would know this.

Eikōn—sometimes in its diminutive form *eikonion*—was the word which was used for a *portrait* in Greek. There is a papyrus letter from a soldier lad called Apion to his father Epimachus. Near the end he writes: "I send you a little portrait (*eikonion*) of myself painted by Euctemon." It is the nearest equivalent in ancient Greek to our word *photograph*. But this word had still another use. When a legal document was drawn up, such as a receipt or an IOU, it always included a description of the chief characteristics and distinguishing marks of the contracting parties, so that there could be no mistake. The Greek word for such a description is *eikōn*. The *eikōn*, therefore, was a kind of brief summary of the personal characteristics and distinguishing marks of the contracting parties. So, then, to the very simplest Paul is saying, "You know how if you enter into a legal agreement, there is included an *eikōn*, a description by which you may be recognized. Jesus is the portrait of God. In him you see the personal characteristics and the distinguishing marks of God. If you want to see what God is like, look at Jesus."

(ii) The other word Paul uses is in verse 19. He says that Jesus is the *plērōma* of God. *Plērōma* means *fullness, completeness*. This is the word which is needed to complete the picture. Jesus is not simply a sketch of God or a summary and more than a lifeless portrait of him. In him there is nothing left out; he is the full revelation of God, and nothing more is necessary.

III. WHAT JESUS CHRIST IS TO CREATION

Colossians 1: 15–23 (*continued*)

WE will remember that according to the Gnostics the work of creation was carried out by an inferior god, ignorant of and hostile to the true God. It is Paul's teaching that God's agent in creation is the Son and in this passage he has four things to say of the Son in regard to creation.

(i) He is the firstborn of all creation (*Colossians* 1: 15). We must be very careful to attach the right meaning to this phrase. As it stands in English it might well mean the Son was the first person to be created, but in Hebrew and Greek thought the word *firstborn* (*prōtotokos*) has only very indirectly a time significance. There are two things to note. *Firstborn* is very commonly a title of *honour*. Israel, for instance, as a nation is the firstborn son of God (*Exodus* 4: 22). The meaning is that the nation of Israel is the most favoured child of God. Second, we must note that *firstborn* is a title of the *Messiah*. In *Psalm* 89: 27, as the Jews themselves interpreted it, the promise regarding the Messiah is "I will make him my firstborn, higher than the kings of the earth." Clearly *firstborn* is not used in a time sense at all, but in the sense of special honour. So when Paul says of the Son that he is the *firstborn* of all creation, he means that the highest honour which creation holds belongs to him. If we wish to keep the time sense and the honour sense combined, we may translate the phrase: "He was begotten before all creation."

(ii) It was by the Son that all things were created (verse 16). This is true of things in heaven and things in earth, of things seen and unseen. The Jews themselves, and even more the Gnostics, had a highly-developed system of angels. With the Gnostics that was only to be expected with their long series of intermediaries between man and God. Thrones, lordships, powers and authorities were different grades of angels having their places in different spheres of the seven heavens. Paul dismisses them all with complete indifference. He is in effect saying to the Gnostics, "You give a great place in your thinking to angels. You rate Jesus Christ merely as one of them. So far from that, he created them." Paul lays it down that the agent of God in creation is no inferior, ignorant and hostile secondary god, but the Son himself.

(iii) It was for the Son that all things were created (verse 17). The Son is not only the agent of creation, he is also the goal of creation. That is to say, creation was created to be his and that in its worship and its love he might find his honour and his joy.

(iv) Paul uses the strange phrase: "In him all things hold together." This means that not only is the Son the agent of creation in the beginning and the goal of creation in the end, but between the beginning and the end, during time as we know it, it is he who holds the world together. That is to say, all the laws by which this world is order and not chaos are an expression of the mind of the Son. The law of gravity and the rest, the laws by which the universe hangs together, are not only scientific laws but also divine.

So, then, the Son is the beginning of creation, and the end of creation, and the power who holds creation together, the Creator, the Sustainer, and the Final Goal of the world.

IV. WHAT JESUS CHRIST IS TO THE CHURCH

Colossians 1: 15–23 (*continued*)

PAUL sets out in verse 18 what Jesus Christ is to the Church; and he distinguishes four great facts in that relationship.

(i) He is *the head of the body,* that is, of the Church. The Church is the body of Christ, that is, the organism through which he acts and which shares all his experiences. But, humanly speaking, the body is the servant of the head and is powerless without it. So Jesus Christ is the guiding spirit of the Church; it is at his bidding that the Church must live and move. Without him the Church cannot think the truth, cannot act correctly, cannot decide its direction. There are two things combined here. There is the idea of *privilege*. It is the privilege of the Church to be the instrument through which Christ works. There is the idea of *warning*. If a man neglects or abuses his body, he can make it unfit to be the servant of the great purposes of his mind; so by indisciplined and careless living the Church can unfit herself to be the instrument of Christ, who is her head.

(ii) He is *the beginning of the Church*. The Greek word for beginning is *archē,* which means *beginning* in a double sense. It means not only first in the sense of time, as, for instance, A is the beginning of the alphabet and 1 is the beginning of the series of numbers. It means first in the sense of the source from which something came, the moving power which set something in operation. We will see more clearly what Paul is getting at, if we remember what he has just said. *The world* is the *creation* of Christ; and *the Church* is the *new creation* of Christ.

> She is his new creation
> By water and the word.

Christ is the source of the Church's life and being and the director of her continued activity.

(iii) He is *the firstborn from among the dead*. Here Paul comes back to the event which was at the centre of all the thinking and belief and experience of the Early Church—the Resurrection. Christ is not merely someone who lived and died and of whom we read and learn. He is someone who, because of his Resurrection, is alive for evermore and whom we meet and experience, not a dead hero nor a past founder, but a living presence.

(iv) The result of all this is that *he has the supremacy in all things*. The Resurrection of Jesus Christ is his title to supreme lordship. By his Resurrection he has shown that he has conquered every opposing power and that there is nothing in life or in death which can bind him.

So there are four great facts about Jesus Christ in his relationship to the Church, which now we can put in order. He is the living Lord; he is the source and origin of the Church; he is the constant director of the Church; and he is the Lord of all, by virtue of his victory over death.

V. WHAT JESUS CHRIST IS TO ALL THINGS

Colossians 1: 15–23 (*continued*)

IN verses 19 and 20 Paul sets down certain great truths about the work of Christ for the whole universe.

(i) The object of his coming was *reconciliation*. He came to heal the breach and bridge the chasm between God and man. We must note one thing quite clearly and always retain it in our memories. The initiative in reconciliation was with God. The New Testament never talks of God being reconciled to men, but always of men being reconciled to God. God's attitude to men was love, and it was never anything else. Sometimes a theology is preached which implies that something that Jesus did changed God's attitude from wrath into love. There is no justification in the New Testament for any such view. It was God who began the whole process of salvation. It was because God so *loved* the world that he sent his Son. His one object in sending his Son into this world was to woo men back to himself and, as Paul puts it, to reconcile all things to himself.

(ii) The medium of reconciliation was *the blood of the Cross*. The dynamic of reconciliation was the death of Jesus Christ. What does Paul mean? He means exactly what he said in *Romans* 8: 32: "He who did not spare his own Son, but gave him up for us all, will he not also give us all things with him?" In the death of Jesus, God is saying to us, "I love you like

that. I love you enough to see my Son suffer and die for you."
The Cross is the proof that there is no length to which the
love of God will refuse to go in order to win men's hearts;
and a love like that demands an answering love. If the Cross
will not waken love in men's hearts, nothing will.

(iii) We must note that Paul says that in Christ God was
reconciling *all things* to himself. The Greek is a neuter (*panta*).
The point is that the reconciliation of God extends not only to
all persons but to all creation, animate and inanimate. The
vision of Paul was a universe in which not only the people but
the very things were redeemed. This is an amazing thought.
There is no doubt that Paul was thinking of the Gnostics. We
will remember that they, regarding matter as essentially and
incurably evil, therefore regarded the world as evil. But, as
Paul sees it, the world is not evil. It is God's world and shares
in the universal reconciliation.

There is a lesson and a warning here. Too often in Christianity there has been suspicion of the world. "Earth is a desert
drear." We remember the story of the Puritan. Someone said
to him, as they walked along the road, "That's a lovely flower".
And the Puritan answered, "I have learned to call nothing
lovely in this lost and sinful world." So far from being
Christian, that attitude is in fact heresy. It was the very attitude
of the Gnostic heretics who threatened to destroy the faith.
This is God's world and it is a redeemed world, for in some
amazing way God in Christ was reconciling the whole universe
of men and living creatures and even inanimate things to
himself.

(iv) The passage ends with a curious little phrase. Paul says
that this reconciliation extended not only to things on earth
but also to things in heaven. How was it that any reconciliation
was necessary for heavenly things? This has exercised the
ingenuity of many commentators; let us look at some of
the explanations.

(*a*) It has been suggested that even the heavenly places and
the angels there were under sin and needed to be reconciled
to God. In *Job* we read: "His angels he charges with error"

(*Job* 4: 18). "The heavens are not clean in his sight" (*Job* 15: 15). So it is suggested that even the angelic beings needed the reconciliation of the Cross.

(*b*) Origen, the great universalist, thought that the phrase referred to the devil and his angels and he believed that in the end even they would be reconciled to God through the work of Jesus Christ.

(*c*) It has been suggested that when Paul said that the reconciling work of Christ extended to all things in earth and in heaven, he did not mean anything definite but was simply using a magnificent and sonorous phrase in which the complete adequacy of the reconciling work of Christ was set out.

(*d*) The most interesting suggestion was made by Theodoret and followed by Erasmus. It was that the point is not that the heavenly angels were reconciled to God, but that they were reconciled to *men*. The suggestion is that the angels were angry with men for what they had done to God and wished to destroy them; and the work of Christ took away their wrath when they saw how much God still loved men.

However these things may be, this much is certain, God's aim was to reconcile men to himself in Jesus Christ, the medium by which he did so was the death of Christ which proved that there were no limits to his love, and that reconciliation extends to all the universe, earth and heaven alike.

VI. THE AIM AND OBLIGATION OF RECONCILIATION

Colossians 1: 15–23 (*continued*)

IN verses 21 to 23 are set out the aim and the obligation of reconciliation.

(i) The aim of reconciliation is *holiness*. Christ carried out his sacrificial work of reconciliation in order to present us to God consecrated and irreproachable. It is easy to twist the idea of the love of God and to say, "Well, if God loves me like this and wishes nothing but reconciliation, sin does not matter. I can do what I like and God will still love me." The reverse is true. The fact that a man is loved does not give him *carte blanche* to do as he likes; it lays upon him the greatest obligation in the world, the obligation of being worthy of that love. In one sense the love of God makes things easy, for it takes away our fear of him and assures us that we are no longer criminals at the bar of judgment, certain of nothing but condemnation. But in another sense it makes things agonizingly and almost impossibly difficult, for it lays upon us this ultimate obligation of seeking to be worthy of that love.

(ii) Reconciliation has another kind of obligation, that of standing fast in the faith and never abandoning the hope of the gospel. Reconciliation demands that through sunshine and through shadow we should never lose confidence in the love of God. Out of the wonder of reconciliation are born the strength of unshakable loyalty and the radiance of unconquerable hope.

THE PRIVILEGE AND THE TASK

Colossians 1 : 24–29

Now I rejoice in my sufferings for you, and in my flesh, for the sake of his body, I fill up what is lacking in the afflictions of Christ. By his body, I mean the Church, of which I was made a servant, according to the office which God gave me to exercise for your sakes. That office is to make the word of God fully known, that secret which has remained hidden throughout all the ages and the generations, but which has now been made manifest to God's dedicated people; for God desired to make known to them how great was the glorious wealth among the Gentiles of this secret now revealed, and that secret is, Christ in you, your glorious hope. It is that Christ whom we proclaim, warning every man, and teaching every man in all wisdom, that we may present every man complete in Christ. That is the end for which I toil, striving with his energy, which works mightily within me.

PAUL begins this passage with a daring thought. He thinks of the sufferings through which he is passing as completing the sufferings of Jesus Christ himself. Jesus died to save his Church; but the Church must be upbuilt and extended; it must be kept strong and pure and true; therefore, anyone who serves the Church by widening her borders, establishing her faith, saving her from errors, is doing the work of Christ. And if such service involves suffering and sacrifice, that affliction is filling up and sharing the very suffering of Christ. To suffer in the service of Christ is not a penalty but a privilege, for it is sharing in his work.

Paul sets out the very essence of the task which has been given him by God. That task was to bring to men a new discovery, a secret kept throughout the ages and the generations and now revealed. This was that the glorious hope of the gospel was not only for the Jews but for all men everywhere. Paul's great contribution to the Christian faith was that he took Christ to the Gentiles and destroyed for ever the idea that God's love and mercy were the property of any one people or any one nation. That is why Paul is in a special sense our saint and our apostle. Had it not been for him Christianity might have become nothing wider than a new Judaism, and we and all other Gentiles might never have received it.

So Paul sets down his great aim. It is to warn *every man,* and to teach *every man,* and to present *every man* complete in Christ.

The *Jew* would never have agreed that God had any use for every man; he would have refused to accept that he was the God of the Gentiles. This idea would have seemed incredible and even blasphemous. The *Gnostic* would never have agreed that every man could be warned and taught and presented complete to God. He believed that the knowledge necessary for salvation was so involved and difficult that it must be the possession of the spiritual aristocracy and the chosen few. E. J. Goodspeed quotes a passage from Walter Lipman's *Preface to Morals*: "As yet no teacher has ever appeared who was wise enough to know how to teach his wisdom to all mankind. In fact, the great teachers have attempted nothing so utopian. They were quite well aware how difficult for most men is wisdom, and they have confessed frankly that the perfect life was for the select few. It is arguable, in fact, that the very idea of teaching the highest wisdom to all men is the recent notion of a humanitarian and romantically democratic age, and that it is quite foreign to the thought of all great teachers." It has always been the case that men have openly or tacitly agreed that wisdom is not for every one.

The fact is that the only thing in this world which is for every man is Christ. It is not every man who can be a thinker. There are gifts which are not granted to every man. Not every man can master every craft, or even every game. There are those who are colour-blind and to whom the loveliness of art means nothing. There are those who are tone-deaf and for whom the glory of music does not exist. Not every man can be a writer or a student or a preacher or a singer. Even human love at its highest is not granted to all men. There are gifts a man will never possess; there are privileges a man will never enjoy; there are heights of this world's attainment which a man will never scale; but to every man there is open the good news of the gospel, the love of God in Christ Jesus and the transforming power which can bring holiness into life.

LOVE'S STRUGGLE

Colossians 2: 1

> I want you to know how great a struggle I am going through for you, and for the people of Laodicaea, and for all those who have never seen me face to face.

HERE is a brief lifting of the curtain and a poignant glimpse into Paul's heart. He is going through a struggle for these Christians whom he had never seen but whom he loved.

He associates the Laodicaeans with the Colossians, and speaks of all those who had never seen his face. He is thinking of the Christians in that group of three towns in the Lycus valley, Laodicaea, Hierapolis and Colosse (see p. 91) and picturing them in his mind's eye.

The word he uses for *struggle* is a vivid word; it is *agōn,* from which comes our own word *agony.* Paul is fighting a hard battle for his friends. We must remember that, when he wrote this letter, he was in prison in Rome, awaiting judgment and almost certain condemnation. What then was his struggle?

(i) It was a struggle in prayer. He must have longed to go to Colosse himself. He must have longed to face the false teachers and deal with their arguments and recall those who were straying from the truth. But he was in prison. There had come a time when there was nothing left to do but to pray; what he could not do himself, he must leave to God. So Paul wrestled in prayer for those whom he could not see. When time and distance and circumstance separate us from those whom we long to help, there is always one way left to help them and that is the way of prayer.

(ii) It may well be that there was another struggle going on in Paul's mind. He was a human being with all a man's natural problems. He was in prison, awaiting trial before Nero, and the issue was almost certainly death. It would have been easy to play the coward and abandon the truth for the sake of safety. Paul well knew that such a desertion would be disastrous in its consequences. If the young Churches knew that Paul had denied Christ, the heart would be taken from them and it would be the end of Christianity for many. His struggle was not for himself alone; it was also for those whose eyes were fixed upon him as their leader and father in the faith. We do well to remember that in any situation there are those who are watching us; and that our action will either confirm or destroy their faith. Our struggle is never for ourselves alone; always the honour of Christ is in our hands and the faith of others in our keeping.

THE MARKS OF THE FAITHFUL CHURCH (i)

Colossians 2: 2–7

My struggle is that their hearts may be encouraged, that they may be united together in love, that they may come to all the wealth of the assured ability to take the right decision in any situation, to the knowledge of that truth which only God's own may know, I mean of Christ, in whom are hidden all the treasures of wisdom and of knowledge.

I say this so that no one may lead you into error by false reasoning with persuasive arguments. For, even if I am absent from you in the body, I am with you in spirit, happy when I see you maintaining your ranks and the solid bulwark of your faith in Christ.

So, then, as you have received Christ Jesus the Lord, live your life in him. Continue to remain firmly rooted, and go on being built up in him. Continue to be established more and more firmly in the faith, as you were taught it, and to overflow with thanksgiving.

HERE is Paul's prayer for the Church, and in it we distinguish the great marks which should distinguish a living and faithful Church.

(i) It should be a Church of *courageous hearts*. Paul prays that their hearts may be *encouraged*. The word which he uses is *parakalein*. Sometimes that word means to *comfort*, sometimes to *exhort*, but always at the back of it there is the idea of enabling a person to meet some difficult situation with confidence and with gallantry. One of the Greek historians uses it in a most interesting and suggestive way. There was a Greek regiment which had lost heart and was utterly dejected. The general sent a leader to talk to it to such purpose that courage was reborn and a body of dispirited men became fit again for heroic action. That is what *parakalein* means here. It is Paul's prayer that the Church may be filled with that courage which can cope with any situation.

(ii) It should be a Church in which the members are *knit together in love*. Without love there is no real Church. Methods of Church government and ritual are not what matter. These things change from time to time and from place to place. The one mark which distinguishes a true Church is love for God and for the brethren. When love dies, the Church dies.

(iii) It should be a Church *equipped with every kind of wisdom*. Paul here uses three words for wisdom.

(*a*) In verse 2 he uses *sunesis,* which the Revised Standard Version translates *understanding*. We have already seen that *sunesis* is what we might call *critical knowledge*. It is the ability to assess any situation and decide what practical course of action is necessary within it. A real Church will have the practical knowledge of what to do whenever action is called for.

(*b*) He says that in Jesus are hid all the treasures of *wisdom* and *knowledge*. Wisdom is *sophia* and knowledge is *gnōsis*. These two words do not simply repeat each other; there is a difference between them. *Gnōsis* is the power, almost intuitive and instinctive, to grasp the truth when we see it and hear it. But *sophia* is the power to confirm and to commend the truth with wise and intelligent argument, once it has been intuitively grasped. *Gnōsis* is that by which a man grasps the truth; *sophia* is that by which a man is enabled to give a reason for the hope that is in him.

So, then, the real Church will have the clear-sighted wisdom which can act for the best in any given situation; the wisdom which can instinctively recognize and grasp the truth when it sees it; and the wisdom which can make the truth intelligible to the thinking mind, and persuasively commend it to others.

All this wisdom, says Paul, is *hidden* in Christ. The word he uses for hidden is *apokruphos*. His very use of that word is a blow aimed at the Gnostics. *Apokruphos* means *hidden from the common gaze,* and therefore *secret*. We have seen that the Gnostics believed that a great mass of elaborate knowledge was necessary for salvation. That knowledge they set down in their books which they called *apokruphos* because they were barred to the ordinary man. By using this one word Paul is saying, "You Gnostics have your wisdom hidden from ordinary people; we too have our knowledge, but it is not hidden in unintelligible books; it is hidden in Christ and therefore open to all men everywhere." The truth of Christianity is not a secret which is hidden but a secret which is revealed.

THE MARKS OF THE FAITHFUL CHURCH (ii)

Colossians 2: 2–7 (*continued*)

(iv) The true Church must have *the power to resist seductive teaching.* It must be such that men cannot beguile it with *enticing words. Enticing words* translates the Greek word *pithanologia.* This was a word of the law-courts; it was the word used for the persuasive power of a lawyer's arguments, which could enable the criminal to escape his just punishment. The true Church should have such a grip of the truth that it is unmoved by seductive arguments.

(v) The true Church should have in it *a soldier's discipline.* As the Revised Standard Version has it, Paul is glad to hear of the *order* and of the *firmness* of the faith of the Colossians. These two words present a vivid picture, for they are both military words. The word translated *order* is *taxis*, which means a *rank* or an ordered arrangement. The Church should be like an ordered army, with every man in his appointed place, ready and willing to obey the word of command. The word translated *firmness* is *stereōma*, which means a solid *bulwark*, an immovable *phalanx.* It describes an army set out in an unbreakable square, solidly immovable against the shock of the enemy's charge. Within the Church there should be disciplined order and strong steadiness, like the order and steadiness of a trained and disciplined body of troops.

(vi) In the true Church *life must be in Christ.* Its members must walk in Christ; their whole lives must be lived in his conscious presence. They must be *rooted* and *built* in him. There are two pictures here. The word used for *rooted* is the word which would be used of a tree with its roots deep in the soil. The word used for *built* is the word which would be used of a house erected on a firm foundation. Just as the great tree is deep-rooted in the soil and draws its nourishment from it, so the Christian is rooted in Christ, the source of his life and strength. Just as the house stands fast because it is built on strong foundations, so the Christian life is resistant to any storm because it is founded on the strength of Christ. Christ is alike the source of the Christian's life and the foundation of his stability.

(vii) The true Church *holds fast to the faith which it has received*. It never forgets the teaching about Christ which it has been taught. This does not mean a frozen orthodoxy in which all adventure of thought is heresy. We have only to remember how in *Colossians* Paul strikes out new lines in his thinking about Jesus Christ to see how far that was from his intention. But it does mean that there are certain beliefs which remain the foundation and do not change. Paul might travel down new pathways of thought but he always began and ended with the unchanging and unchangeable truth that Jesus Christ is Lord.

(viii) The distinguishing mark of the true Church is *an abounding and overflowing gratitude*. Thanksgiving is the constant and characteristic note of the Christian life. As J. B. Lightfoot put it: "Thanksgiving is the end of all human conduct, whether observed in words or works." The one concern of the Christian is to tell in words and to show in life his gratitude for all that God has done for him in nature and in grace. Epictetus was not a Christian, but that little, old, lame slave who became one of the great moral teachers of paganism, wrote: "What else can I, a lame old man, do but sing hymns to God? If, indeed, I were a nightingale, I would be singing as a nightingale; if a swan, as a swan. But, as it is, I am a rational being, therefore I must be singing hymns of praise to God. This is my task; I do it, and will not desert this post, as long as it may be given me to fill it; and I exhort you to join with me in this same song." (Epictetus, *Discourses* 1.16.21). The Christian will always praise God from whom all blessings flow.

ADDITIONS TO CHRIST

Colossians 2: 8–23

Beware lest there will be anyone who will carry you off as his spoil, by insisting on the necessity of a so-called philosophy, which is, in fact, an empty delusion, a philosophy which has been handed down by human tradition, and which is concerned with the elements of this world, and not with Christ; for in him there dwells the fullness of the divine nature; and you have found this fullness in him who is the head of every power and authority. In him you have been circumcised with a circumcision not made by man's hands, a circumcision which consists in putting off the whole of that part of you which is dominated by sinful human nature, which you were able to do by the circumcision which belongs to Christ. You were buried with him in the act of baptism, and in that act you were raised with him through your faith in the effective working of God, who raised him from the dead. God made you alive with him, when you were dead in your sins and were still uncircumcised Gentiles. He forgave you all your sins, and wiped out the charge-list which set out all your self-admitted debts, a charge-list which was based on the ordinances of the law and was in direct opposition to you. He nailed it to his Cross and put it right out of sight. He stripped the powers and authorities of all their power and publicly put them to shame, and, through the Cross, led them captive in his triumphal train.

Let no one take you to task in matters of food or drink, or with regard to yearly festivals and monthly new moons and weekly sabbaths. These are only the shadow of things to come; the real substance belongs to Christ. Let no one rob you of your prize by walking in ostentatious humility in the worship of angels, making a parade of the things he has seen, vainly inflated with pride because he is dominated by his sinful human nature and not holding fast to the head, from whom the whole body, supplied and held together by the joints and muscles, increases with the increase which only God can give.

If you died with Christ to the elements of this world, why do you continue to submit yourselves to their rules and regulations, as if you were still living in a world without God? "Handle not! Taste not! Touch not!" are their slogans. These are rules which are humanly taught and humanly imposed, and they are rules which deal with things which are destined for decay as soon as they are used.

These things have a reputation for wisdom, with their self-imposed devotion and their flaunting humility and their stern treatment of the body, but they have no kind of value in remedying the indulgence of sinful human nature.

THERE can be no doubt that for us this is one of the most difficult passages Paul ever wrote. For those who heard or read it for the first time it would be crystal clear. The trouble is that it is packed from beginning to end with allusions to the false teaching which was threatening to wreck the Colossian Church. We do not know precisely what that teaching was. Therefore the allusions are obscure and we can only guess. But every sentence and every phrase would go straight home to the minds and the hearts of the Colossians.

It is so difficult that we propose to treat it in a slightly different way from our usual practice. We have set it out as a whole, in what is more of a paraphrase than a translation. We will take out its leading ideas, for it is possible to see the main lines of the false teaching which was troubling Colosse; and then, after we have looked at it as a whole, we shall examine it in more detail in shorter sections.

One thing clear is that the false teachers wished the Colossians to accept what can only be called *additions to Christ*. They were teaching that Jesus Christ himself is not sufficient; that he was not unique; that he was one among many manifestations of God; and that it was necessary to know and to serve other divine powers in addition to him. We can distinguish five additions to Christ which these false teachers wished to make.

(i) They wished to teach men an additional *philosophy* (verse 8). As they saw it, the simple truth preached by Jesus and preserved in the gospel was not enough. It had to be filled out by an elaborate system of pseudo-philosophical thought which was far too difficult for the simple and which only the intellectual could understand.

(ii) They wished men to accept a system of *astrology* (verse 8). As we shall see, there is a doubt about the meaning but we think it most likely that *the elements of the world* were the elemental spirits of the universe, especially of the stars and the planets. It was the teaching of these false teachers that men were still under these influences and needed a special knowledge, beyond that which Jesus could give, to be liberated from them.

(iii) They wished to impose *circumcision* on Christians (verse 11). Faith was not enough; circumcision had to be added. A badge in the flesh was to take the place of, or at least be an addition to, an attitude of the heart.

(iv) They wished to lay down *ascetic rules and regulations* (verses 16, 20–23). They wished to introduce all kinds of rules and regulations about what a man might eat and drink and about what days he must observe as festivals and fasts. All the old Jewish regulations—and more—were to be brought back.

(v) They wished to introduce *the worship of angels* (verse 18). They were teaching that Jesus was only one of many inter-mediaries between God and man and that all these inter-mediaries must receive their worship.

It can be seen that here there is a mixture of Gnosticism and Judaism. The intellectual knowledge and the astrology come direct from Gnosticism; the asceticism and the rules and regulations from Judaism. What happened was this. We have seen that the Gnostics believed that all kinds of special know-ledge, beyond the gospel, was needed for salvation. There were Jews who joined forces with the Gnostics and declared that the special knowledge required was none other than the knowledge which Judaism could give. This explains why the teaching of the Colossians' false teachers combined the beliefs of Gnosti-cism with the practices of Judaism.

The one thing certain is that the false teachers taught that Jesus Christ and his teaching and work were not in themselves sufficient for salvation. Let us now take the passage section by section.

TRADITIONS AND THE STARS

Colossians 2: 8–10

Beware lest there will be anyone who will carry you off as his spoil, by insisting on the necessity of a so-called philosophy, which is, in fact, an empty delusion, a philosophy which has been handed down by human tradition, and which is concerned with the elements of this world and not with Christ; for in him there dwells the fullness of the divine nature; and you have found this fullness in him who is the head of every power and authority.

PAUL begins by drawing a vivid picture of the false teachers. He speaks of anyone who will *carry you off as his spoil*. The word is *sulagōgein* and could be used of a slave-dealer carrying away the people of a conquered nation into slavery. To Paul it was an amazing and a tragic thing that men who had been liberated (*Colossians* 1: 12–14), could contemplate submitting themselves to a new and disastrous slavery.

These men offer a philosophy which they declare is necessary in addition to the teaching of Christ and the words of the gospel.

(i) It is a philosophy which has been *handed down by human tradition*. The Gnostics were in the habit of claiming that their special teaching was teaching which had been told by word of mouth by Jesus, sometimes to Mary, sometimes to Matthew, and sometimes to Peter. They did, in fact, say that there were things which Jesus never told the crowd and communicated only to the chosen few. The charge Paul makes against these teachers is that their teaching is a human thing; it has no basis in Scripture. It is a product of the human mind; and not a message of the Word of God. To speak like this is not to drift into fundamentalism or submit to a tyranny of the written word, but to hold that no teaching can be Christian teaching which is at variance with the basic truths of Scripture and with the Word of God.

(ii) It is a philosophy which has to do with the *elements of this world*. This is a much-discussed phrase of which the meaning is still in doubt. The word for elements is *stoicheia* and *stoicheia* has two meanings.

(*a*) It means literally *things which are set out in a row*. It is, for instance, the word for a file of soldiers. But one of its commonest meanings is the letters of the alphabet, no doubt because they form a series which can be set out in a row. Because *stoicheia* can mean the letters of the alphabet, it can also very commonly mean *elementary instruction in any subject.* We still speak of learning the A B C of a subject, when we mean taking the first steps in it. It is possible that this is the meaning here. Paul may be saying, "These false teachers claim that they are giving you knowledge which is very advanced and very profound. In point of fact it is knowledge which is uninstructed and rudimentary because at the best it is knowledge of the human mind. The real knowledge, the real fullness of God, is in Jesus Christ. If you listen to these false teachers, so far from receiving deep spiritual knowledge, you are simply slipping back into rudimentary instruction which you should have left behind long ago."

(*b*) *Stoicheia* has a second meaning. It means the *elemental spirits of the world,* and especially the spirits of the stars and planets. There are still people today who take astrology seriously. They wear signs of the zodiac charms and read newspaper columns which tell what is forecast for them in the stars. But it is almost impossible for us to realize how dominated the ancient world was by the idea of the influence of the elemental spirits and the stars. Astrology was then, as someone has said, the queen of the sciences. Even men so great as Julius Caesar and Augustus, so cynical as Tiberius, so level-headed as Vespasian would take no step without consulting the stars. Alexander the Great believed implicitly in the influence of the stars. Men and women believed that their whole lives were fixed by them. If a man was born under a fortunate star all was well; if he was born under an unlucky star, he could not look for happiness; if any undertaking was to have a chance of success, the stars must be observed. Men were the slaves of the stars.

There was one possibility of escape. If men knew the right pass-words and the right formulae, they might escape from this fatalistic influence of the stars; and a great part of the secret teaching of Gnosticism and of kindred faiths and philosophies was knowledge which claimed to give the devotee escape from the power of the stars; and in all probability that was what the false teachers of Colosse were offering. They were saying, "Jesus Christ is all very well, he can do much for you; but he cannot enable you to escape from your subjection to the stars. We alone have the secret knowledge which can enable you to do that." Paul, sufficiently the child of his age to believe in these elemental spirits, answers: "You need nothing but Christ to overcome any power in the universe; for in him is nothing less than the fullness of God and he is the head of every power and authority, for he created them."

The Gnostic teachers offered an additional philosophy; Paul insisted on the triumphant adequacy of Christ to overcome any power in any part of the universe. You cannot at one and the same time believe in the power of Christ and the influence of the stars.

THE REAL AND THE UNREAL CIRCUMCISION

Colossians 2: 11, 12

> In him you have been circumcised with a circumcision not made by man's hands, a circumcision which consists in putting off the whole of that part of you which is dominated by sinful human nature, which you were able to do by the circumcision which belongs to Christ. You were buried with him in the act of baptism and in that act you were raised with him through your faith in the effective working of God, who raised him from the dead.

THE false teachers were demanding that Gentile Christians should be circumcised for circumcision was the badge of God's chosen people. God, they argued, had said to Abraham, "This is my covenant, which you shall keep, between me and you, and your descendants after you; Every male among you shall be circumcised" (*Genesis* 17: 10).

All through the history of Israel there had been two views

of circumcision. There was the view of those who said that in itself it was enough to put a man right with God. It did not matter whether an Israelite was a good man or a bad man; all that mattered was that he was an Israelite and that he had been circumcised.

But the great spiritual leaders of Israel and the great prophets took a very different view. They insisted that circumcision was only the outward mark of a man who was inwardly dedicated to God. They used the very word in an adventurous sense. They talked of uncircumcised *lips* (*Exodus* 6: 12), of a *heart* which was circumcised or uncircumcised (*Leviticus* 26: 41; *Ezekiel* 44: 7, 9; *Deuteronomy* 30: 6); of the uncircumcised ear (*Jeremiah* 6: 10). To them being circumcised did not mean having a certain operation carried out on a man's flesh but having a change effected in his life. Circumcision was, indeed, the badge of a person dedicated to God; but the dedication lay not in the cutting of the flesh but in the excision from his life of everything which was against the will of God.

That was the answer of the prophets centuries before: and that was still Paul's answer to the false teachers. He said to them, "You demand circumcision; but you must remember that circumcision does not mean simply the removal of the foreskin from a man's body; it means the putting off of that whole part of his human nature which sets him at variance with God." Then he went on: "Any priest can circumcise a man's foreskin; only Christ can bring about that spiritual circumcision which means cutting away from a man's life everything which keeps him from being God's obedient child."

Paul goes further. For him this was not theory but fact. "That very act," he said, "has already happened to you in baptism." When we think of his view of baptism we must remember three things. In the early Church, as today in the mission field and even in the Church extension areas, men were coming straight out of heathenism into Christianity. They were knowingly and deliberately leaving one way of life for another; and making in the act of baptism a conscious decision. This was of course, before the days of infant baptism which did not and could not come until the Christian family had become a reality.

Baptism in the time of Paul was three things. It was *adult* baptism; it was *instructed* baptism; and, wherever possible, it was baptism by *total immersion*. Therefore the symbolism of baptism was manifest. As the waters closed over the man's head, it was as if he died; as he rose up again from the water, it was as if he rose to new life. Part of him was dead and gone for ever; he was a new man risen to a new life.

But, it must be noted, that symbolism could become a reality only under one condition. It could become real only when a man believed intensely in the life and death and resurrection of Jesus Christ. It could only happen when a man believed in the effective working of God which had raised Jesus Christ from the dead and could do the same for him. Baptism for the Christian was in truth a dying and a rising again, because he believed that Christ had died and risen again and that he was sharing the experience of his Lord.

"You speak about circumcision," said Paul. "The only true circumcision is when a man dies and rises with Christ in baptism, in such a way that it is not part of his body which is cut away but his whole sinful self which is destroyed, and he is filled with newness of life and the very holiness of God."

TRIUMPHANT FORGIVENESS

Colossians 2: 13–15

God made you alive with Christ, when you were dead in your sins and were still uncircumcised Gentiles. He forgave you all your sins and wiped out the charge-list which set out all your self-admitted debts, a charge-list which was based on the ordinances of the law and which was in direct opposition to you. He nailed it to his Cross and put it right out of sight. He stripped the powers and authorities of all their power and publicly put them to shame and, through the Cross, led them captive in his triumphal train.

ALMOST all great teachers have thought in pictures; and here Paul uses a series of vivid pictures to show what God in Christ has done for men. The intention is to show that Christ has done all that can be done and all that need be done, and that there is no need to bring in any other intermediaries for the full salvation of men. There are three main pictures here.

(i) Men were dead in their sins. They had no more power than dead men either to overcome sin or to atone for it. Jesus Christ by his work has liberated men both from the power and from the consequences of sin. He has given them a life so new that it can only be said that he has raised them from the dead. Further, it was the old belief that only the Jews were dear to God, but this saving power of Christ has come even to the uncircumcised Gentile. The work of Christ is a work of power, because it put life into dead men; it is a work of grace, because it reached out to those who had no reason to expect the benefits of God.

(ii) But the picture becomes even more vivid. As the Authorized Version has it, Jesus Christ blotted out the handwriting of ordinances which was against us; as we have translated it, he wiped out the charge-list which set out all our self-admitted debts, a charge-list based on the ordinances of the law. There are two Greek words here on which the whole picture depends.

(a) The word for *handwriting* or *charge-list* is *cheirographon*. It literally means an *autograph*; but its technical meaning— a meaning which everyone would understand—was a note of hand signed by a debtor acknowledging his indebtedness. It was almost exactly what we call an I.O.U. Men's sins had piled up a vast list of debts to God and it could be said that men definitely acknowledged that debt. More than once the Old Testament shows the children of Israel hearing and accepting the laws of God and calling down curses on themselves should they fail to keep them (*Exodus* 24: 3; *Deuteronomy* 27: 14–26). In the New Testament we find the picture of the Gentiles as having, not the written law of God which the Jews had, but the unwritten law in their hearts and the voice of conscience speaking within (*Romans* 2: 14, 15). Men were in debt to God because of their sins and they knew it. There was a self-confessed indictment against them, a charge-list which, as it were, they themselves had signed and admitted as accurate.

(*b*) The word for wiping out is the Greek verb *exaleiphein*. To understand that word is to understand the amazing mercy of God. The substance on which ancient documents were written was either papyrus, a kind of paper made of the pith of the bulrush, or vellum, a substance made of the skins of animals. Both were fairly expensive and certainly could not be wasted. Ancient ink had no acid in it; it lay on the surface of the paper and did not, as modern ink usually does, bite into it. Sometimes a scribe, to save paper, used papyrus or vellum that had already been written upon. When he did that, he took a sponge and wiped the writing out. Because it was only on the surface of the paper, the ink could be wiped out as if it had never been. God, in his amazing mercy, banished the record of our sins so completely that it was as if it had never been; not a trace remained.

(*c*) Paul goes on. God took that indictment and nailed it to the Cross of Christ. It used to be said that in the ancient world when a law or an ordinance was cancelled, it was fastened to a board and a nail was driven clean through it. But it is doubtful if that was the case and if that is the picture here. Rather it is this—on the Cross of Christ the indictment that was against us was itself crucified. It was executed and put clean out of the way, so that it might never be seen again. Paul seems to have searched human activity to find a series of pictures which would show how completely God in his mercy destroyed the condemnation that was against us.

Here indeed is grace. And that new era of grace is further underlined in another rather obscure phrase. The charge-list had been *based on the ordinances of the law*. Before Christ came men were under law and they broke it because no man can perfectly keep it. But now law is banished and grace has come. Man is no longer a criminal who has broken the law and is at the mercy of God's judgment; he is a son who was lost and can now come home to be wrapped around with the grace of God.

(iii) One other great picture flashes on the screen of Paul's mind. Jesus has stripped the powers and authorities and made them his captives. As we have seen, the ancient world believed in all kinds of angels and in all kinds of elemental spirits. Many of these spirits were out to ruin men. It was they who were responsible for demon-possession and the like. They were hostile to men. Jesus conquered them for ever. He *stripped* them; the word used is the word for stripping the weapons and the armour from a defeated foe. Once and for all Jesus broke their power. He put them to open shame and led them captive in his triumphant train. The picture is that of the triumph of a Roman general. When a Roman general had won a really notable victory, he was allowed to march his victorious armies through the streets of Rome and behind him followed the kings and the leaders and the peoples he had vanquished. They were openly branded as his spoils. Paul thinks of Jesus as a conqueror enjoying a kind of cosmic triumph, and in his triumphal procession are the powers of evil, beaten for ever, for every one to see.

In these vivid pictures Paul sets out the total adequacy of the work of Christ. Sin is forgiven and evil is conquered; what more is necessary? There is nothing that Gnostic knowledge and Gnostic intermediaries can do for men—Christ has done it all already.

RETROGRESSION

Colossians 2: 16–23

Let no one take you to task in matters of food or drink, or with regard to yearly festivals and monthly new moons and weekly sabbaths. These are only the shadow of things to come; the real substance belongs to Christ. Let no one rob you of your prize by walking in ostentatious humility in the worship of angels, making a parade of the things which he has seen, vainly inflated with pride because he is dominated by his sinful human nature and not holding fast to the head, from which the whole body, supplied and held together by the joints and muscles, increases with the increase which God alone can give.

If you died with Christ to the elements of this world, why do you continue to submit yourselves to their rules and regulations, as if you were still living in a world without God? "Handle not! Taste not! Touch not!" are their slogans. These are rules which are humanly taught and humanly imposed, and they are rules which deal with things which are destined for decay as soon as they are used. These things have a reputation for wisdom, with their self-imposed devotion and their flaunting humility and their stern treatment of the body, but they have no kind of value in remedying the indulgencies of sinful human nature.

THIS passage has certain basic Gnostic ideas intertwined all through it. In it Paul is warning the Colossians not to adopt certain Gnostic practices, on the grounds that to do so would be not progress but rather retrogression in the faith. Behind it lie four Gnostic practices.

(i) There is Gnostic *asceticism* (verses 16 and 21). There is the teaching which involves a whole host of regulations about what can and can not be eaten and drunk. In other words there is a return to all the food laws of the Jews, with their lists of things clean and unclean. As we have seen, the Gnostics considered all matter to be essentially evil. If matter is evil, then the body is evil. If the body is evil, two opposite conclusions may be drawn. (a) If the body is essentially evil, it does not matter what we do with it. Being evil it can be used or abused in any way, and it makes no difference. (b) If the body is evil, it must be kept down; it must be beaten and starved and its every impulse chained down. That is to say, Gnosticism could issue either in complete immorality or in rigid asceticism. It is the rigid asceticism with which Paul is dealing here.

In effect he says, "Have nothing to do with people who

identify religion with laws about what you may or may not eat or drink." Jesus himself had said that it made no difference what a man ate or drank (*Matthew* 15: 10–20; *Mark* 7: 14–23). Peter had to learn to cease to talk about clean and unclean foods (*Acts* 10). Paul uses an almost crude phrase which repeats in different words what Jesus had already said. He says, "These things perish as they are used" (verse 22). He means exactly what Jesus did when he said that food and drink are eaten and digested, and then excreted from the body, and flushed away down the drain (*Matthew* 15: 17; *Mark* 7: 19). Food and drink are so unimportant that they are destined for decay as soon as they are eaten. The Gnostics wished to make religion a thing of regulations about eating and drinking; and there are still those who are more concerned with rules about food than about the charity of the gospel.

(ii) There is the Gnostic and the Jewish *observation of days* (verse 16). They observed yearly feasts and monthly new moons and weekly sabbaths. They drew out lists of days which specially belonged to God, on which certain things must be done and certain things must not be done. They identified religion with ritual.

Paul's criticism of this stress on days is quite clear and logical. He says, "You have been rescued from all this tyranny of legal rules. Why do you want to enslave yourself all over again? Why do you want to go back to Jewish legalism and abandon Christian freedom?" The spirit which makes Christianity a thing of regulations is by no means dead yet.

(iii) There are the Gnostic *special visions*. The Authorized Version in verse 18 speaks of the false teacher "intruding into those things which he hath not seen." That is a mistranslation. The correct translation should be "making a parade of the things which he has seen." The Gnostic prided himself upon special visions of secret things which were not open to the eyes of ordinary men and women. No one will deny the visions of the mystics, but there is always danger when a man begins to think that he has attained a height of holiness which enables him to see what common men—as he calls them—cannot see;

and the danger is that men will so often see, not what God sends them, but what they want to see.

(iv) There is the *worship of angels* (verses 18 and 20). As we have seen, the Jews had a highly-developed doctrine of angels and the Gnostics believed in all kinds of intermediaries. They worshipped these, while the Christian knows that worship must be kept for God and for Jesus Christ.

Paul makes four criticisms of all this.

(i) He says that this kind of thing is only a shadow of truth; the real truth is in Christ (verse 17). That is to say, a religion which is founded on eating and drinking certain kinds of food and drink and abstaining from others, a religion which is founded on Sabbath observance and the like, is only a shadow of real religion; real religion is fellowship with Christ.

(ii) He says that there is such a thing as a false humility (verses 18 and 23). When they talked of the worship of angels, both the Gnostics and the Jews would have justified it by saying that God is so great and high and holy that we can never have direct access to him and must be content to pray to the angels. But the great truth that Christianity preaches is, in fact, exactly that the way to God is open to the humblest and the simplest person.

(iii) He says that this can lead to sinful pride (verses 18 and 23). The man who is meticulous in his observance of special days, who keeps all the food laws and who practises ascetic abstinence is in very grave danger of thinking himself specially good and of looking down on other people. And it is a basic truth of Christianity that no man who thinks himself good is really good, least of all the man who thinks himself better than other people.

(iv) He says that this is a return to unchristian slavery instead of Christian freedom (verse 20) and that in any event, it does not free a man from fleshly lusts but only keeps them on the leash (verse 23). Christian freedom comes not from restraining desires by rules and regulations but from the death of evil desires and the springing to life of good desires by virtue of Christ being in the Christian and the Christian in Christ.

THE RISEN LIFE

Colossians 3: 1–4

If then you were raised with Christ, set your hearts on the things which are above, where Christ is seated at the right hand of God. Have a mind all of whose thoughts are fixed on the things which are above, not upon the things on earth. For you died and your life is hidden with Christ in God. Whenever Christ, your life, shall appear, then you too shall appear with him in glory.

THE point Paul is making here is this. In baptism the Christian dies and rises again. As the waters close over him, it is as if he was buried in death; as he emerges from the waters, it is like being resurrected to a new life. Now, if that is so, the Christian must rise from baptism a different man. Wherein is the difference? It lies in the fact that now the thoughts of the Christian must be set on the things which are above. He can no longer be concerned with the trivial passing things of earth; he must be totally concerned with the eternal verities of heaven.

We must note carefully what Paul means by that. He is certainly not pleading for an other-worldliness in which the Christian withdraws himself from all the work and activities of this world and does nothing but contemplate eternity. Immediately after this Paul goes on to lay down a series of ethical principles which make it quite clear that he expects the Christian to go on with the work of this world and to maintain all its normal relationships. But there will be this difference— from now on the Christian will view everything against the background of eternity and no longer live as if this world was all that mattered.

This will obviously give him a new set of values. Things which the world thought important, he will no longer worry about. Ambitions which dominated the world, will be powerless to touch him. He will go on using the things of the world but he will use them in a new way. He will, for instance, set giving above getting, serving above ruling, forgiving above avenging. The Christian's standard of values will be God's not men's.

And how is this to be accomplished? The life of the Christian is hid with Christ in God. There are at least two vivid pictures here.

(i) We have seen repeatedly that the early Christians regarded baptism as a dying and a rising again. When a man was dead and buried, the Greeks very commonly spoke of him as being *hidden in the earth*; but the Christian had died a spiritual death in baptism and he is not hidden in the earth, but *hidden in Christ*. It was the experience of the early Christians that the very act of baptism wrapped a man round with Christ.

(ii) There may well be a word play here which a Greek would recognize at once. The false teachers called their books of so-called wisdom *apokruphoi*, the books that were hidden from all except from those who were initiated. Now the word which Paul uses to say that our lives are *hidden* with Christ in God is part of the verb *apokruptein*, from which the adjective *apokruphos* comes. Undoubtedly the one word would suggest the other. It is as if Paul said, "For you the treasures of wisdom are hidden in your secret books; for us Christ is the treasury of wisdom and we are hidden in him."

There is still another thought here. The life of the Christian is *hidden* with Christ in God. That which is hidden is concealed; the world cannot recognize the Christian. But Paul goes on: "The day is coming when Christ will return in glory and then the Christian, whom no one recognized, will share that glory and it will be plain for all to see." In a sense Paul is saying—and saying truly—that some day the verdicts of eternity will reverse the verdicts of time and the judgments of God will overturn the judgments of men.

CHRIST OUR LIFE

Colossians 3: 1–4 (*continued*)

IN verse 4 Paul gives to Christ one of the great titles of devotion. He calls him *Christ our life*. Here is a thought which was very dear to the heart of Paul. When he was writing to the Philippians, he said, "For me to live is Christ" (*Philippians* 1: 21). Years before, when he was writing to the Galatians, he had said, "It is no longer I who live but Christ who lives in me" (*Galatians* 2: 20). As Paul saw it, to the Christian Christ is the most important thing in life; more, he *is* life.

This is the kind of peak of devotion which we can only dimly understand and only haltingly and imperfectly express. Sometimes we say of a man, "Music is his life—Sport is his life—He lives for his work." Such a man finds life and all that it means in music, in sport, in work, as the case may be. For the Christian, Christ is his life.

And here we come back to where this passage started— that is precisely why the Christian sets his mind and heart on the things which are above and not on the things of this world. He judges everything in the light of the Cross and in the light of the love which gave itself for him. In the light of that Cross the world's wealth and ambitions and activities are seen at their true value; and, the Christian is enabled to set his whole heart on the things which are above.

THE THINGS WHICH LIE BEHIND

Colossians 3: 5–9a

So, then, put to death these parts of you which are earthly— fornication, uncleanness, passion, evil desire, the desire to get more than you ought—for this is idol worship; and because of these things the wrath of God comes upon those who are disobedient. It was amongst these things that you once spent your lives. when you lived among them; but now you must divest yourselves of all these things—anger. temper. malice. slander. foul talk which issues from your mouth. Do not lie to one another.

HERE this letter makes the change that Paul's letters always make; after the theology comes the ethical demand. Paul could think more deeply than any man who ever tried to express the Christian faith; he could travel along uncharted pathways of thought; he could scale the heights of the human mind, where even the best equipped theologian finds it hard to follow him; but always at the end of his letters he turns to the practical consequences of it all. He always ends with an uncompromising and crystal clear statement of the ethical demands of Christianity in the situation in which his friends are at the moment.

Paul begins with a vivid demand. The New Testament never hesitates to demand with a certain violence the complete elimination of everything which is against God. The Authorized Version translates the first part of this section: "Mortify your members which are upon earth." In seventeenth-century English that was clear enough: but it has lost its force in modern language. Nowadays *to mortify the flesh* means rather to practise ascetic discipline and self-denial. And that is not enough. What Paul is saying is, "Put to death every part of your self which is against God and keeps you from fulfilling his will." He uses the same line of thought in *Romans* 8: 13: "If you live according to the flesh you will die, but if by the Spirit you put to death the deeds of the body you will live." It is exactly the same line of thought as that of Jesus when he demanded that a man should cut off a hand or a foot, or tear out an eye when it was leading him into sin (*Matthew* 5: 29, 30).

We may put this in more modern language, as C. F. D. Moule expresses it. The Christian must kill self-centredness and regard as dead all private desires and ambitions. There must be in his life a radical transformation of the will and a radical shift of the centre. Everything which would keep him from fully obeying God and fully surrendering to Christ must be surgically excised.

Paul goes on to list some of the things which the Colossians must cut right out of life.

Fornication and *uncleanness* must go. Chastity was the one completely new virtue which Christianity brought into the world. In the ancient world sexual relationships before marriage and outside marriage were the normal and accepted practice. The sexual appetite was regarded as a thing to be gratified, not to be controlled. That is an attitude which is not unfamiliar today, although often it is supported by specious arguments. In his autobiography, *Memory to Memory,* Sir Arnold Lunn has a chapter on Cyril Joad, the well-known philosopher, whom he knew well. In his pre-Christian days Joad could write: "Birth control (he meant the use of contraceptives) increases the possibilities of human pleasure. In enabling the pleasures of sex to be tasted without its penalties it has removed the most formidable deterrent not only to regular but to irregular sexual intercourse . . . The average clergyman is shocked and outraged by the prospect of shameless, harmless and unlimited pleasure which birth control offers to the young, and, if he can stop it, he will." Towards the end of his life Joad came back to religion and returned to the family of the Church; but it was not without a struggle, and it was the insistence of the Christian Church on sexual purity which kept him so long from making the final decision. "It's a big step," he said, "and I can't persuade myself that the very severe attitude to sex which the Church thinks it necessary to adopt is really justified." The Christian ethic insists on chastity, regarding the physical relationship between the sexes as something so precious that indiscriminate use of it in the end spoils it.

There was *passion* and *evil desire*. There is a kind of person who is the slave of his passions (*palkos*) and who is driven by the desire for the wrong things (*epithumia*).

There is the sin which the Revised Standard Version calls *covetousness* (*pleonexia*). *Pleonexia* is one of the ugliest of sins but while it is quite clear what it means, it is by no means so easy to find a single word to translate it. It comes from two Greek words; the first half of the word is from *pleon* which means more and the second half is from *echein* which means *to have*. *Pleonexia* is basically *the desire to have more*. The Greeks themselves defined it as insatiate desire and said that you might as easily satisfy it as you might fill with water a bowl with a hole in it. They defined it as the sinful desire for what belongs to others. It has been described as ruthless self-seeking. Its basic idea is the desire for that which a man has no right to have. It is, therefore, a sin with a very wide range. If it is the desire for money, it leads to theft. If it is the desire for prestige, it leads to evil ambition. If it is the desire for power, it leads to sadistic tyranny. If it is the desire for a person, it leads to sexual sin. C. F. D. Moule well describes it as "the opposite of the desire to give."

Such a desire, says Paul, is idolatry. How can that be? The essence of idolatry is the desire to get. A man sets up an idol and worships it because he desires to get something from it. To quote C. F. D. Moule, "idolatry is an attempt to use God for man's purposes, rather than to give oneself to God's service." The essence of idolatry is, in fact, the desire to have more. Or to come at it another way, the man whose life is dominated by the desire to get things has set up things in the place of God—and that precisely is idolatry.

Upon all such things the wrath of God must fall. The wrath of God is simply the rule of the universe that a man will sow what he reaps and that no one ever escapes the consequences of his sin. The wrath of God and the moral order of the universe are one and the same thing.

THE THINGS WHICH MUST BE LEFT BEHIND

Colossians 3: 5–9a (*continued*)

IN verse 8 Paul says that there are certain things of which the Colossians must strip themselves. The word he uses is the word for *putting off clothes*. There is here a picture from the life of the early Christian. When the Christian was baptized, he put off his old clothes when he went down into the water and when he emerged he put on a new and pure white robe. He divested himself of one kind of life and put on another. In this passage Paul speaks of the things of which the Christian must divest himself, and in verse 12 he will continue the picture and speak of the things which the Christian must put on. Let us look at these things one by one.

The Christian must put off *anger* and *temper*. The two words are *orgē* and *thumos,* and the difference between them is this. *Thumos* is a blaze of sudden anger which is quickly kindled and just as quickly dies. The Greeks likened it to a fire amongst straw, which quickly blazed and just as quickly burned itself out. *Orgē* is anger which has become inveterate; it is long-lasting, slow-burning anger, which refuses to be pacified and nurses its wrath to keep it warm. For the Christian the burst of temper and the long-lasting anger are alike forbidden.

There is *malice*. The word we have so translated is *kakia*; it is a difficult word to translate, for it really means that viciousness of mind from which all the individual vices spring. It is all-pervading evil.

Christians must put off *slander* and *foul talk* and they must not *lie to one another*. The word for slander is *blasphēmia,* which the Authorized Version translates *blasphemy. Blasphēmia* is insulting and slanderous speaking in general; when that insulting speech is directed against God, it becomes blasphemy. In this context it is much more likely that what is forbidden is slanderous talk against one's fellow-men. The word we have translated *foul talk* is *aischrologia*; it could well mean *obscene language*. These last three forbidden things have all to do with speech. And when we turn them into positive commands instead of negative prohibitions, we find three laws for Christian speech.

(i) Christian speech must be *kind*. All slanderous and malicious talking is forbidden. The old advice still stands which says that before we repeat anything about anyone we should ask three questions: "Is it true? Is it necessary? Is it kind?" The New Testament is unsparing in its condemnation of the gossiping tongues which poison truth.

(ii) Christian speech must be *pure*. There can never have been a time in history when so much filthy language is used as today. And the tragedy is that many people have become so habituated to unclean talk that they are unaware that they are using it. The Christian should never forget that he will give account for every idle word he speaks.

(iii) Christian speech must be *true*. Dr. Johnson believed that there are far more falsehoods told unaware than deliberately; and he believed that a child should be checked when he deviates in the smallest detail from the truth. It is easy to distort the truth; an alteration in the tone of voice or an eloquent look will do it; and there are silences which can be as false and misleading as any words.

Christian speech must be kind and pure and honest to all men and in all places.

THE UNIVERSALITY OF CHRISTIANITY

Colossians 3: 9b–13

> Strip off the old self with all its activities. Put on the new self, which is ever freshly renewed until it reaches fullness of knowledge, in the likeness of its creator. In it there is neither Greek nor Jew, circumcision nor uncircumcision, barbarian, Scythian, slave nor free man, but Christ is all in all. So then, as the chosen of God, dedicated and beloved, clothe yourself with a heart of pity, kindness, humility, gentleness, patience. Bear with one another, and, if anyone has a ground of complaint against someone else, forgive each other; as the Lord has forgiven you, so you must forgive each other.

WHEN a man becomes a Christian, there ought to be a complete change in his personality. He puts off his old self and puts on a new self, just as the candidate for baptism puts off his old clothes and puts on the new white robe. We very often evade the truth on which the New Testament insists, that a Christianity which does not change a man is most imperfect. Further, this change is progressive. This new creation is a continual renewal. It makes a man grow continually in grace and knowledge until he reaches that which he was meant to be—manhood in the image of God.

One of the great effects of Christianity is that it destroys the barriers. In it there is neither Greek nor Jew, circumcised nor uncircumcised, barbarian, Scythian, slave nor free man. The ancient world was full of barriers. The Greek looked down on the barbarian; and to the Greek any man who did not speak Greek was a barbarian, which literally means a man who says "bar-bar." The Greek was the aristocrat of the ancient world and he knew it. The Jew looked down on every other nation. He belonged to God's chosen people and the other nations were fit only to be fuel for the fires of hell. The Scythian was notorious as the lowest of the barbarians; more barbarian than the barbarians, the Greeks called him; little short of being a wild beast, Josephus calls him. He was proverbially the savage, who terrorized the civilized world with his bestial atrocities. The slave was not even classified in ancient law as a human being; he was merely a living tool, with no rights of his own. His master could thrash or brand or maim or even kill him at his caprice; he had not even the right of marriage. There could be no fellowship in the ancient world between a slave and a free man.

In Christ all these barriers were broken down. J. B. Lightfoot reminds us that one of the greatest tributes paid to Christianity was paid not by a theologian but by a master linguist. Max Müller was one of the great experts of the science of language. In the ancient world no one was interested in foreign languages, apart from Greek. The Greeks were the scholars and they would never have deigned to study a barbarian tongue. The science of language is a new science and the desire to know other languages a new desire. Max Müller wrote: "Not till that word *barbarian* was struck out of the dictionary of mankind, and replaced by *brother,* not till the right of all nations of the world to be classed as members of one genus or kind was recognized, can we look even for the first beginnings of our science of language . . . This change was effected by Christianity." It was Christianity which drew men together sufficiently to make them wish to know each other's languages.

T. K. Abbott points out how this passage shows in summary fashion the barriers which Christianity destroyed.

(i) It destroyed the barriers which came from birth and nationality. Different nations, who either despised or hated each other, were drawn into the one family of the Christian Church. Men of different nationalities, who would have leaped at each other's throats, sat in peace beside each other at the Table of the Lord.

(ii) It destroyed the barriers which came from ceremonial and ritual. Circumcised and uncircumcised were drawn together in the one fellowship. To a Jew a man of any other nation was unclean; when he became a Christian, every man of every nation became a brother.

(iii) It destroyed the barriers between the cultured and the uncultured. The Scythian was the ignorant barbarian of the ancient world; the Greek was the aristocrat of learning. The uncultured and the cultured came together in the Christian Church. The greatest scholar in the world and the simplest son of toil can sit in perfect fellowship in the Church of Christ.

(iv) It destroyed the barrier between class and class. The slave and the free man came together in the Church. More than that, in the Early Church it could, and did, happen that the slave was the leader of the Church and the master the humble member. In the presence of God the social distinctions of the world become irrelevant.

THE GARMENTS OF CHRISTIAN GRACE

Colossians 3: 9b–13 (*continued*)

PAUL moves on to give his list of the great graces with which the Colossians must clothe themselves. Before we study the list in detail, we must note two very significant things.

(i) Paul begins by addressing the Colossians as *chosen of God, dedicated* and *beloved*. The significant thing is that every one of these three words originally belonged, as it were, to the Jews. They were the chosen people; they were the dedicated nation; they were the beloved of God. Paul takes these three precious words which had once been the possession of Israel and gives them to the Gentiles. Thereby he shows that God's love and grace have gone out to the ends of the earth, and that there is no "most favoured nation" clause in his economy.

(ii) It is most significant to note that every one of the graces listed has to do with personal relationships between man and man. There is no mention of virtues like efficiency or cleverness, not even of diligence or industry—not that these things are unimportant. But the great basic Christian virtues are those which govern human relationships. Christianity is community. It has on its divine side the amazing gift of peace with God and on its human side the triumphant solution of the problem of living together.

Paul begins with *a heart of pity*. If there was one thing the ancient world needed it was mercy. The sufferings of animals were nothing to it. The maimed and the sickly went to the wall. There was no provision for the aged. The treatment of the idiot and the simple-minded was unfeeling. Christianity brought mercy into this world. It is not too much to say that everything that has been done for the aged, the sick, the weak in body and in mind, the animal, the child, the woman has been done under the inspiration of Christianity.

There is kindness (*chrēstotēs*). Trench calls this a lovely word for a lovely quality. The ancient writers defined *chrēstotēs* as the virtue of the man whose neighbour's good is as dear to him as his own. Josephus uses it as a description of Isaac, the man who dug wells and gave them to others because he would not fight about them (*Genesis* 26: 17–25). It is used of wine which has grown mellow with age and lost its harshness. It is the word used when Jesus said, "My yoke is *easy*." (*Matthew* 11: 30). Goodness by itself can be stern; but *chrēstotēs* is the goodness which is kind, that type of goodness which Jesus used to the sinning woman who anointed his feet (*Luke* 7: 37–50). No doubt Simon the Pharisee was a good man; but Jesus was more than good, he was *chrēstos*. The Rheims version translates it *benignity*. The Christian is marked by a goodness which is a kindly thing.

There is *humility* (*tapeinophrosunē*). It has often been said that humility was a virtue created by Christianity. In classical Greek there is no word for humility which has not some tinge of servility; but Christian humility is not a cringing thing. It is based on two things. First, on the divine side, it is based on the awareness of the *creatureliness* of humanity. God is the Creator, man the creature, and in the presence of the Creator the creature cannot feel anything else but humility. Second, on the human side, it is based on the belief that all men are the sons of God; and there is no room for arrogance when we are living among men and women who are all of royal lineage.

There is *gentleness* (*praotēs*). Long ago Aristotle had defined *praotēs* as the happy mean between too much and too little anger. The man who has *praotēs* is the man who is so self-controlled, because he is God-controlled, that he is always angry at the right time and never angry at the wrong time. He has at one and the same time the strength and the sweetness of true gentleness.

There is *patience* (*makrothumia*). This is the spirit which never loses its patience with its fellow-men. Their foolishness and their unteachability never drive it to cynicism or despair; their insults and their ill-treatment never drive it to bitterness or wrath. Human patience is a reflection of the divine patience which bears with all our sinning and never casts us off.

There is the *forbearing and the forgiving spirit*. The Christian forbears and forgives; and he does so because a forgiven man must always be forgiving. As God forgave him, so he must forgive others, for only the forgiving can be forgiven.

THE PERFECT BOND

Colossians 3: 14–17

On top of all these things, clothe yourselves with love which is the perfect bond; and let the peace of God be the decider of all things within your hearts, for it is to that peace you were called, so that you might be united in one body. May the word of Christ dwell richly in you with all wisdom. Continue to teach and to admonish each other with psalms and hymns and spiritual songs, singing to God with gratitude in your hearts. And whatever you may be doing in word or in deed, do all things in the name of the Lord Jesus, giving thanks to God the Father through him.

To the virtues and the graces Paul adds one more—what he calls *the perfect bond of love*. Love is the binding power which holds the whole Christian body together. The tendency of any body of people is sooner or later to fly apart; love is the one bond which will hold them together in unbreakable fellowship.

Then Paul uses a vivid picture. "Let the peace of God be the decider of all things within your heart." Literally what he says is, "Let the peace of God be the umpire in your heart." He uses a verb from the athletic arena; it is the word that is used of the umpire who settled things in any matter of dispute. If the peace of Jesus Christ is the umpire in any man's heart, then, when feelings clash and we are pulled in two directions at the same time, the decision of Christ will keep us in the way of love and the Church will remain the one body it is meant to be. The way to right action is to appoint Jesus Christ as the arbiter between the conflicting emotions in our hearts; and if we accept his decisions, we cannot go wrong.

It is interesting to see that from the beginning the Church was a singing Church. It inherited that from the Jews, for Philo tells us that often they would spend the whole night in hymns and songs. One of the earliest descriptions of a Church service we possess is that of Pliny, the Roman governor of Bithynia, who sent a report of the activities of the Christians to Trajan, the Roman Emperor, in which he said, "They meet at dawn to sing a hymn to Christ as God." The gratitude of the Church has always gone up to God in praise and song.

Finally, Paul gives the great principle for living that

everything we do or say should be done and said in the name of Jesus. One of the best tests of any action is: "Can we do it, calling upon the name of Jesus? Can we do it, asking for his help?" One of the best tests of any word is: "Can we speak it and in the same breath name the name of Jesus? Can we speak it, remembering that he will hear?" If a man brings every word and deed to the test of the presence of Jesus Christ, he will not go wrong.

THE PERSONAL RELATIONSHIPS OF THE CHRISTIAN

Colossians 3: 18–4: 1

Wives, be submissive to your husbands, as is fitting in the Lord. Husbands, love your wives and do not treat them harshly.

Children, obey your parents in all things, for this is well-pleasing in the Lord. Fathers, do not irritate your children, that they may not lose heart.

Slaves, obey in all things those who are your human masters, not only when you are watched, like those whose only desire is to please men, but in sincerity of heart, reverencing the Lord. Whatever you do, work at it heartily, as if you were doing it for the Lord and not for men; and never forget that you will receive from the Lord your just recompense, even your share in the inheritance. Show yourselves the slaves of the Lord Christ. He who does wrong will be paid back for the wrong that he has done, and there is no respect of persons.

Masters, on your part provide for your slaves treatment which is just and equitable, and remember that you too have a master in heaven.

HERE the ethical part of the letter becomes more and more practical. Paul turns to the working out of Christianity in the everyday relationships of life and living. Before we begin to study the passage in some detail, we must note two great general principles which lie behind it and determine all its demands.

(i) The Christian ethic is an ethic of *reciprocal obligation*.

It is never an ethic on which all the duties are on one side. As Paul saw it, husbands have as great an obligation as wives; parents have just as binding a duty as children; masters have their responsibilities as much as slaves.

This was an entirely new thing. Let us take the cases one by one and look at them in the light of this new principle.

Under Jewish law a woman was a thing, the possession of her husband, just as much as his house or his flocks or his material goods. She had no legal rights whatever. For instance, under Jewish law, a husband could divorce his wife for any cause, while a wife had no rights whatever in the initiation of divorce; and the only grounds on which a divorce might be awarded her were if her husband developed leprosy, became an apostate or ravished a virgin. In Greek society a respectable woman lived a life of entire seclusion. She never appeared on the streets alone, not even to go marketing. She lived in the women's apartments and did not join her menfolk even for meals. From her there was demanded complete servitude and chastity; but her husband could go out as much as he chose and could enter into as many relationships outside marriage as he liked without incurring any stigma. Under both Jewish and Greek laws and custom all the privileges belonged to the husband and all the duties to the wife.

In the ancient world children were very much under the domination of their parents. The supreme example was the Roman *Patria Potestas,* the law of the father's power. Under it a parent could do anything he liked with his child. He could sell him into slavery; he could make him work like a labourer on his farm; he had even the right to condemn his child to death and to carry out the execution. All the privileges and rights belonged to the parent and all the duties to the child.

Most of all this was the case in slavery. The slave was a thing in the eyes of the law. There was no such thing as a code of working conditions. When the slave was past his work, he could be thrown out to die. He had not even the right to marry, and if he cohabited and there was a child, the child belonged to the master, just as the lambs of the flock belonged to the shepherd. Once again all the rights belonged to the master and all the duties to the slave.

The Christian ethic is one of mutual obligation, in which the rights and the obligations rest with every man. It is an ethic of mutual responsibility; and, therefore, it becomes an ethic where the thought of privilege and rights falls into the background and where the thought of duty and obligation becomes paramount. The whole direction of the Christian ethic is not to ask: "What do others owe to me?" but, "What do I owe to others?"

(ii) The really new thing about the Christian ethic of personal relationships is that all relationships are *in the Lord*. The whole of the Christian life is lived in Christ. In any home the tone of personal relationships must be dictated by the awareness that Jesus Christ is an unseen but ever-present guest. In any parent-child relationship the dominating thought must be the Fatherhood of God; and we must try to treat our children as God treats his sons and daughters. The thing which settles any master and servant relationship is that both are servants of the one Master, Jesus Christ. The new thing about personal relationships in Christianity is that Jesus Christ is introduced into them all.

THE MUTUAL OBLIGATION

Colossians 3: 18–4: 1 (*continued*)

LET us look briefly at each of these three spheres of human relationships.

(i) The wife is to be submissive to her husband; but the husband is to love his wife and to treat her with all kindness. The practical effect of the marriage laws and customs of ancient times was that the husband became an unquestioned dictator and the wife little more than a servant to bring up his children and to minister to his needs. The fundamental effect of this Christian teaching is that marriage becomes a *partnership*. It becomes something which is entered into not merely for the convenience of the husband, but in order that both husband and wife may find a new joy and a new completeness in each other. Any marriage in which everything is done for the convenience of one of the partners and where the other exists simply to gratify the needs and desires of the first, is not a Christian marriage.

(ii) The Christian ethic lays down the duty of the child to respect the parental relationship. But there is always a problem in the relationship of parent and child. If the parent is too easy-going, the child will grow up indisciplined and unfit to face life. But there is a contrary danger. The more conscientious a parent is, the more he is likely always to be correcting and rebuking the child. Simply because he wishes the child to do well, he is always on his top.

We remember, for instance, the tragic question of Mary Lamb, whose mind was ultimately unhinged: "Why is it that I never seem to be able to do anything to please my mother?" We remember the poignant statement of John Newton: "I know that my father loved me—but he did not seem to wish me to see it." There is a certain kind of constant criticism which is the product of misguided love.

The danger of all this is that the child may become discouraged. Bengel speaks of "the plague of youth, a broken spirit (*Fractus animus pestis iuventutis*)." It is one of the tragic facts of religious history that Luther's father was so stern to him that Luther all his days found it difficult to pray: "Our Father." The word *father* in his mind stood for nothing but severity. The duty of the parent is discipline, but it is also encouragement. Luther himself said, "Spare the rod and spoil the child. It is true. But beside the rod keep an apple to give him when he does well."

Sir Arnold Lunn, in *Memory to Memory,* quotes an incident about Field-Marshal Montgomery from a book by M. E. Clifton James. Montgomery was famous as a disciplinarian—but there was another side to him. Clifton James was his official "double" and was studying him during a rehearsal for D-Day. "Within a few yards of where I was standing, a very young soldier, still looking sea-sick from his voyage, came struggling along gamely trying to keep up with his comrades in front. I could imagine that, feeling as he did, his rifle and equipment must have been like a ton weight. His heavy boots dragged in the sand, but I could see that he was fighting hard to conceal his distress. Just when he got level with us he tripped up and fell flat on his face. Half sobbing, he heaved himself up and began to march off dazedly in the wrong direction. Monty went straight up to him and with a quick, friendly smile turned him round. 'This way, sonny. You're doing well—very well. But don't lose touch with the chap in front of you.' When the youngster realized who it was that had given him friendly help, his expression of dumb adoration was a study." It was just because Montgomery combined discipline and encouragement that a private in the Eighth Army felt himself as good as a colonel in any other army.

The better a parent is the more he must avoid the danger of discouraging his child, for he must give discipline and encouragement in equal parts.

THE CHRISTIAN WORKMAN AND THE CHRISTIAN MASTER

Colossians 3: 18–4: 1 (*continued*)

(iii) Paul then turns to the greatest problem of all—the relationship between slave and master. It will be noted that this section is far longer than the other two; and its length may well be due to long talks which Paul had with the runaway slave, Onesimus, whom later he was to send back to his master Philemon.

Paul says things which must have amazed both sides.

He insists that the slave must be a conscientious workman. He is in effect saying that his Christianity must make him a better and more efficient slave. Christianity never in this world offers escape from hard work; it makes a man able to work still harder. Nor does it offer a man escape from difficult situations; it enables him to meet these situations better.

The slave must not be content with eye-service; he must not work only when the overseer's eye is upon him. He must not be the kind of servant, who, as C. F. D. Moule puts it, does not dust behind the ornaments or sweep below the wardrobe. He must remember that he will receive his inheritance. Here was an amazing thing. Under Roman law a slave could not possess any property whatsoever and here he is being promised nothing less than the inheritance of God. He must remember that the time will come when the balance is adjusted and evil-doing will find its punishment and faithful diligence its reward.

The master must treat the slave not like a thing, but like a person, with justice and with the equity which goes beyond justice.

How is it to be done? The answer is important, for in it there is the whole Christian doctrine of work.

The workman must do everything as if he was doing it for Christ. We do not work for pay or for ambition or to satisfy an earthly master; we work so that we can take every task and offer it to Christ. All work is done for God so that his world may go on and his men and women have the things they need for life and living.

The master must remember that he too has a Master—Christ in heaven. He is answerable to God, just as his workmen are answerable to him. No master can say, "This is my business and I will do what I like with it." He must say, "This is God's business. He has put me in charge of it. I am responsible to him." The Christian doctrine of work is that master and man alike are working for God, and that, therefore, the real rewards of work are not assessable in earthly coin, but will some day be given—or withheld—by God.

THE CHRISTIAN'S PRAYER

Colossians 4: 2–4

> Persevere in prayer. Be vigilant in your prayer, and let thanksgiving always be a part of it. And at the same time pray for us, that God may open for us a door for the word, that we may speak the secret of Christ now revealed to his own people, that secret for which I am in bonds, that I may make it manifest to all, as I ought to speak.

PAUL would never write a letter without urging the duty and the privilege of prayer on his friends.

He tells them to persevere in prayer. Even for the best of us, there come times when prayer seems to be unavailing and to penetrate no farther than the walls of the room in which we pray. At such a time the remedy is not to stop but to go on praying; for in the man who prays spiritual dryness cannot last.

He tells them to be vigilant in prayer. Literally the Greek means to be *wakeful*. The phrase could well mean that Paul is telling them not to go to sleep when they pray. Maybe he was thinking of the time on the Mount of Transfiguration when the disciples fell asleep and only when they were awake again saw the glory (*Luke* 9: 32). Or maybe he was thinking of that time in the Garden of Gethsemane when Jesus prayed and his disciples slept (*Matthew* 26: 40). It is true that at the end of a hard day sleep often comes upon us when we try to pray. And even oftener there is in our prayers a kind of tiredness. At such a time we should not try to be long: God will understand the single sentence uttered in the manner of a child too tired to stay awake.

Paul asks their prayers for himself. We must note carefully exactly what it is for which Paul asks. He asks their prayer not so much for himself as for his work. There were many things for which Paul might have asked them to pray—release from prison, a successful outcome to his coming trial, a little rest and peace at the last. But he asks them to pray only that there may be given to him strength and opportunity to do the work which God had sent him into the world to do. When we pray for ourselves and for others, we should not ask release from any task, but rather strength to complete the task which has been given us to do. Prayer should always be for power and seldom for release; for not release but conquest must be the keynote of the Christian life.

THE CHRISTIAN AND THE WORLD

Colossians 4: 5, 6

> Behave yourselves wisely to those who are outside the Church.
> Buy up every possible opportunity.
> Let your speech always be with gracious charm, seasoned with the salt of wit, so that you will know the right answer to give in every case.

HERE are three brief instructions for the life of the Christian in the world.

(i) The Christian must behave himself with wisdom and with tact towards those who are outside the Church. He must of necessity be a missionary; but he must know when and when not to speak to others about his religion and theirs. He must never give the impression of superiority and of censorious criticism. Few people have ever been argued into Christianity. The Christian, therefore, must remember that it is not so much by his words as by his life that he will attract people to, or repel them from, Christianity. On the Christian there is laid the great responsibility of showing men Christ in his daily life.

(ii) The Christian must be a man on the outlook for opportunity. He must buy up every opportunity possible to work for Christ and to serve men. Daily life and work are continually offering men opportunities to witness for Christ and to influence people for him—but there are so many who avoid the opportunities instead of embracing them. The Church is constantly offering its members the opportunity to teach, to sing, to visit, to work for the good of the Christian congregation—and there are so many who deliberately refuse these opportunities instead of accepting them. The Christian should always be on the outlook for the opportunity to serve Christ and his fellow-men.

(iii) The Christian must have charm and wit in his speech so that he may know how to give the right answer in every case. Here is an interesting injunction. It is all too true that Christianity in the minds of many is connected with a kind of sanctimonious dullness and an outlook in which laughter is almost a heresy. As C. F. D. Moule says, this is "a warning not to confuse loyal godliness with graceless insipidity." The Christian must commend his message with the charm and the wit which were in Jesus himself. There is too much of the Christianity which stodgily depresses a man and too little of the Christianity which scintillates with life.

FAITHFUL COMPANIONS

Colossians 4: 7–11

Tychicus, the beloved brother and faithful servant and my fellow-slave in Christ, will inform you all about how things are going with me. I send him to you for this very purpose, that you may know about what is happening to me and that he may encourage your hearts. Along with him I send Onesimus, the faithful and beloved brother, who is one of yourselves. They will inform you about all that has been happening here. Aristarchus, my fellow-prisoner, greets you, and Mark, Barnabas's cousin. (I have given you instructions about him; if he comes to you, give him a welcome.) Jesus, who is called Justus, sends you greetings. These were all converts from the Jewish faith. These alone are my fellow-workers in the work of the Kingdom, men who have been a comfort to me.

THE list of names at the end of this chapter is a list of heroes of the faith. We must remember the circumstances. Paul was in prison awaiting trial and it is always dangerous to be a prisoner's friend, for it is so easy to become involved in the same fate as the prisoner himself. It took courage to visit Paul in his imprisonment and to show that one was on the same side. Let us collect what we know of these men.

There was *Tychicus*. He came from the Roman province of Asia and was most likely the representative of his Church to carry its offering to the poor Christians of Jerusalem (*Acts* 20: 4). To him also was entrusted the duty of bearing to its various destinations the letter we know as the letter to the Ephesians (*Ephesians* 6: 21). There is one rather interesting thing here. Paul writes that Tychicus will tell them all about how things are going with him. This shows how much was left to word of mouth and never set down in Paul's letters at all. In the nature of things the letters could not be very long and they dealt with the problems of faith and conduct which were threatening the Churches. The personal details were left to the bearer of the letter to tell. Tychicus, then, we can describe as the personal envoy of Paul.

There was *Onesimus*. Paul's way of mentioning him is full of lovely courtesy. Onesimus was the runaway slave who had somehow reached Rome and Paul was sending him back to his master Philemon. But he does not call him a runaway slave; he calls him a faithful and beloved brother. When Paul had anything to say about a man, he always said the best that he could.

There was *Aristarchus*. He was a Macedonian from Thessalonica (*Acts* 20: 4). We get only fleeting glimpses of Aristarchus but from these glimpses one thing emerges—he was clearly a good man to have about in a tight corner. He was there when the people of Ephesus rioted in the Temple of Diana and was so much in the forefront that he was captured by the mob (*Acts* 19: 29). He was there when Paul set sail a prisoner for Rome (*Acts* 27: 2). It may well be that he had actually enrolled himself as Paul's slave in order that he might be allowed to make the last journey with him. And now he is here in Rome, Paul's fellow-prisoner. Clearly Aristarchus was a man who was always on the spot when things were at their grimmest. Whenever Paul was in bad trouble Aristarchus was there. The glimpses we have are enough to indicate a really good companion.

There was *Mark*. Of all the characters in the Early Church

he had had the most surprising career. He was so close a friend that Peter could call him his son (1 *Peter* 5: 13); and we know that when he wrote his gospel, it was the preaching material of Peter that he was setting down. On the first missionary journey Paul and Barnabas had taken Mark with them to be their secretary (*Acts* 13: 5); but in the middle of the journey, when things got difficult, Mark quit and went home (*Acts* 13: 13). It was long before Paul could forgive that. When they were about to set out on the second missionary journey, Barnabas once more wished to take Mark with them. But Paul refused to take the quitter again, and on this issue he and Barnabas parted company and never worked together again (*Acts* 15: 36–40). Tradition says that Mark went as a missionary to Egypt and founded the Church at Alexandria. What happened in the interim we do not know; but we do know that he was with Paul in his last imprisonment who had once again come to look on him as a most useful man to have around (*Philemon* 24; 2 *Timothy* 4: 11). Mark was the man who redeemed himself. Here in this brief reference there is an echo of the old, unhappy story. Paul instructs the Church at Colosse to receive Mark and to give him a welcome if he should come. Why does he do that? Doubtless because his Churches looked with suspicion on the man whom Paul had once dismissed as useless for the service of Christ. And now Paul, with his habitual courtesy and thoughtfulness, is making sure that Mark's past will not stand in his way by giving him full approval as one of his trusted friends. The end of Mark's career is a tribute at one and the same time to Mark and to Paul.

Of *Jesus, who was called Justus*, we know nothing but his name.

These were Paul's helps and comforters. We know that it was but a cool welcome that the Jews in Rome gave him (*Acts* 28: 17–29); but there were men with him in Rome whose loyalty must have warmed his heart.

MORE NAMES OF HONOUR

Colossians 4: 12–15

> Epaphras, one of yourselves, the slave of Jesus Christ, greets you.
> He is always wrestling in prayer for you, that you may stand mature
> and fully assured in the faith, engaged in doing the will of God. I bear
> him witness that he has toiled greatly for you and for those in
> Laodicaea and in Hierapolis. Luke, the beloved physician, greets
> you, and so does Demas. Greet the brothers in Laodicaea and
> Nymphas and the Church in their house.

So this honour-roll of Christian workers goes on.

There was *Epaphras*. He must have been the minister of the
Church at Colosse (*Colossians* 1: 7). This passage would seem
to mean that he was, in fact, the overseer of the Churches in
the group of three towns, Hierapolis, Laodicaea and Colosse.
He was a servant of God who prayed and toiled for the people
over whom God had set him.

There was *Luke* the beloved physician, who was with Paul
to the end (2 *Timothy* 4: 11). Was he a doctor, who gave up
what might have been a lucrative career in order to tend Paul's
thorn in the flesh and to preach Christ?

There was *Demas*. It is significant that Demas's name is the
only one to which some comment of praise and appreciation
is not attached. He is Demas and nothing more. There is a story
behind the brief references to Demas in the letters of Paul. In
Philemon 24 he is grouped with the men who are described as
Paul's fellow-labourers. Here in *Colossians* 4: 14 he is simply
Demas. And in the last mention of him (in 2 *Timothy* 4: 10) he
is Demas who has forsaken Paul because he loved this present
world. Surely here we have the faint outlines of a study in
degeneration, loss of enthusiasm and failure in the faith. Here
is one of the men who refused to be remade by Christ.

There was *Nymphas* (the Revised Standard Version has the
feminine, *Nympha*) and the Church of the brothers at
Laodicaea which met in his house. We must remember that
there was no such thing as a special Church building until the

third century. Up to that time the Christian congregations met in the houses of those who were the leaders of the Church. There was the Church which met in the house of Aquila and Prisca in Rome and Ephesus (*Romans* 16: 5; 1 *Corinthians* 16: 19). There was the Church which met in the house of Philemon (*Philemon* 2). In the early days, Church and home were identical: and it is still true that every Christian home should also be a Church of Jesus Christ.

THE MYSTERY OF THE LAODICAEAN LETTER

Colossians 4: 16

> When this letter has been read among you, see to it that it is also read in the Church of the Laodicaeans, and see to it that you read the letter which is on the way to you from Laodicaea.

HERE is one of the mysteries of Paul's correspondence. The letter to Colosse has to be sent on to Laodicaea. And, says Paul, a letter is on the way from Laodicaea to Colosse. What was this Laodicaean letter? There are four possibilities.

(i) It may have been a special letter to the Church at Laodicaea. If so, it is lost, although, as we shall shortly see, an alleged letter to Laodicaea still exists. It is certain that Paul must have written more letters than we possess. We have only thirteen Pauline letters, covering roughly fifteen years. Many letters of his must have been lost, and it may be that the letter to Laodicaea was such a one.

(ii) It may be the letter we know as *Ephesians*. It is well-nigh certain that *Ephesians* was not written to the Church at Ephesus but was an encyclical letter meant to circulate among all the Churches of Asia. It may be that this encyclical had reached Laodicaea and was now on the way to Colosse.

(iii) It may actually be the letter to *Philemon*. That is a real possibility as we try to show in our study of that letter.

(iv) For many centuries there has been in existence an alleged letter of Paul to the Church at Laodicaea. As we have it, it is in Latin; but the Latin is such that it has every sign of being a literal translation of a Greek original. This letter is actually included in the *Codex Fuldensis* of the Latin New Testament which belonged to Victor of Capua and which goes back to the sixth century. This alleged Laodicaean letter can be traced even further back. It was mentioned by Jerome in the fifth century, but Jerome himself said that it was a forgery and that most people agreed that it was not authentic. The letter runs as follows:

Paul an apostle, not by men neither through any man, but through Jesus Christ, to the brothers who are at Laodicaea. Grace be to you and peace from God the Father and from our Lord Jesus Christ.

I thank Christ in every one of my prayers that you remain steadfast in him, and that you persevere in his works, awaiting his promise on the day of judgment. Let not the empty words of certain men seduce you, words of men who try to persuade you that you should turn away from the truth of the gospel which is preached by me . . . (There follows a verse where the text is uncertain).

And now my bonds which I suffer in Christ are plain for all to see; in them I delight and joy. And this will result for me in everlasting salvation, a result which will be brought about by your prayers, and by the help of the Holy Spirit, whether by my life or by my death. For me to live is to be in Christ, and to die is joy. And may he in his mercy bring this very thing to pass in you, that you may have the same love, and that you may be of the one mind.

Therefore, my best-beloved, as you have heard in my presence, so hold to these things and do them in fear of God, and then there will be to you life for eternity; for it is God who works in you. And do without wavering whatever you do.

As for what remains, best-beloved, rejoice in Christ; beware of those who are sordid in their desire for gain. Let all your prayers be made known before God; and be you firm in the mind of Christ.

Do the things which are pure, and true, and modest, and just, and lovely.

Hold fast what you have heard and received into your heart; and you will have peace.

The saints salute you.

The grace of the Lord Jesus Christ be with your spirit.

Cause that this letter be read to the Colossians, and that the letter of the Colossians be read to you.

Such is the alleged letter of Paul to the Laodicaeans. It is clearly made up mainly of phrases taken from *Philippians* with the opening introduction taken from *Galatians*. There can be little doubt that it was the creation of some pious writer who read in *Colossians* that there had been a letter to Laodicaea and who proceeded to compose what he thought such a letter should be. Very few people would accept this ancient letter to the Laodicaeans as a genuine letter of Paul.

We cannot explain the mystery of this letter to the Church at Laodicaea. The most commonly accepted explanation is that the reference is to the circular letter which we know as *Ephesians*; but the suggestion put forward in our study of *Philemon* is even more romantic and very attractive.

THE CLOSING BLESSING

Colossians 4: 17, 18

> And say to Archippus, "See that you complete that piece of service which you have received from the Lord to do."
> Here is my greeting in the handwriting of myself, Paul.
> Remember my bonds.
> Grace be with you.

THE letter closes with an urgent spur to Archippus to be true to a special task which has been given to him. It may be that we can never tell what that task was; it may be that our study of *Philemon* throws light upon it. For the moment we must leave it at that.

To write his letters Paul used a secretary. We know, for instance, that the penman who did the writing of *Romans* was called Tertius (*Romans* 16: 22). It was Paul's custom at the end of a letter to write his signature and his blessing with his own hand—and here he does just that.

"Remember my bonds," he says. Again and again in this series of letters Paul refers to his bonds (*Ephesians* 3: 1; 4: 1; 6: 20; *Philemon* 9). There is no self-pity and no sentimental plea for sympathy. Paul finishes his letter to the Galatians: "I bear on my body the marks of Jesus" (*Galatians* 6: 17). Of course, there is pathos. Alford comments movingly: "When we read of *his chains* we should not forget that they moved over the paper as he wrote (his signature). His hand was chained to the soldier that kept him." But Paul's references to his sufferings are not pleas for sympathy; they are his claims to authority, the guarantees of his right to speak. It is as if he said, "This is not a letter from someone who does not know what the service of Christ means or someone who is asking others to do what he is not prepared to do himself. It is a letter from one who has himself suffered and sacrificed for Christ. My only right to speak is that I too have carried the Cross of Christ."

And so the letter comes to its inevitable end. The end of every one of Paul's letters is grace. He always ended by commending others to that grace which he himself had found sufficient for all things.

THE LETTERS TO THE THESSALONIANS

INTRODUCTION TO THE LETTERS TO
THE THESSALONIANS

PAUL COMES TO MACEDONIA

For anyone who can read between the lines the story of Paul's coming to Macedonia is one of the most dramatic in the book of *Acts*. Luke, with supreme economy of words, tells it in *Acts* 16: 6–10. Short as that narrative is, it gives the impression of a chain of circumstances inescapably culminating in one supreme event. Paul had passed through Phrygia and Galatia and ahead of him lay the Hellespont. To the left lay the teeming province of Asia, to the right stretched the great province of Bithynia; but the Spirit would allow him to enter neither. There was something driving him relentlessly on to the Aegean Sea. So he came to Alexandrian Troas, still uncertain where he ought to go; and then there came to him a vision in the night of a man who cried, "Come over into Macedonia and help us." Paul set sail, and for the first time the gospel came to Europe.

ONE WORLD

At that moment Paul must have seen much more than a continent for Christ. It was in Macedonia that he landed; and Macedonia was the kingdom of Alexander the Great, who had conquered the world and wept because there were no more worlds left to conquer. But Alexander was much more than a military conqueror. He was almost the first universalist. He was more a missionary than a soldier; and he dreamed of one world dominated and enlightened by the culture of Greece. Even so great a thinker as Aristotle had said that it was a plain duty to treat Greeks as free men and orientals as slaves; but Alexander declared that he had been sent by God "to unite, to pacify and to reconcile the whole world." Deliberately he had said that it was his aim "to marry the East to the West." He had dreamed of an Empire in which there was neither Greek nor Jew, barbarian or Scythian, bond or free (*Colossians* 3: 11). It is hard to see how Alexander could have failed to be in Paul's thoughts. Paul left from Alexandrian Troas which was called after Alexander; he came to Macedonia which was Alexander's original kingdom; he worked at Philippi which was called after Philip, Alexander's father; he went on to Thessalonica which was called after Alexander's half-sister. The whole territory was saturated with memories of Alexander; and Paul must surely have thought, not of a country nor of a continent, but of a world for Christ.

PAUL COMES TO THESSALONICA

This sense of the wide-stretching arms of Christianity must have been accentuated when Paul came to Thessalonica. It was a great city. Its original name was Thermai, which means The Hot Springs, and it gave its name to the Thermaic Gulf on which it stood. Six hundred years ago Herodotus had described it as a great city. It has always been a famous harbour. It was there that Xerxes the Persian had his naval base when he invaded Europe; and even in Roman times it was one of the world's great dockyards. In 315 B.C. Cassander had rebuilt the city and renamed it Thessalonica, the name of his wife, who was a daughter of Philip of Macedon and a half-sister of Alexander the Great. It was a free city; that is to say it had never suffered the indignity of having Roman troops quartered within it. It had its own popular assembly and its own magistrates. Its population rose to 200,000 and for a time it was a question whether it or Constantinople would be recognized as the capital of the world. Even today, under the name Salonika, it has 70,000 inhabitants.

But the supreme importance of Thessalonica lay in this— it straddled the Via Egnatia, the Egnatian Road, which stretched from Dyrrachium on the Adriatic to Constantinople on the Bosphorus and thence away to Asia Minor and the East. Its main street was part of the very road which linked Rome with the East. East and West converged on Thessalonica; it was said to be "in the lap of the Roman Empire." Trade poured into her from East and West, so that it was said, "So long as nature does not change, Thessalonica will remain wealthy and prosperous."

It is impossible to overstress the importance of the arrival of Christianity in Thessalonica. If Christianity was settled there, it was bound to spread East along the Egnatian Road until all Asia was conquered and West until it stormed even the city of Rome. The coming of Christianity to Thessalonica was crucial in the making of it into a world religion.

PAUL'S STAY AT THESSALONICA

The story of Paul's stay at Thessalonica is in *Acts* 17: 1–10. Now, for Paul, what happened at Thessalonica was of supreme importance. He preached in the synagogue for three Sabbaths (*Acts* 17: 2) which means that his stay there could not have been much more than three weeks in length. He had such tremendous success that the Jews were enraged and raised so much trouble that Paul had to be smuggled out, in peril of his life, to Beroea. The same thing happened in Beroea (*Acts* 17: 10–12) and Paul had to leave Timothy and Silas behind and make his escape to Athens. What exercised his mind was this. He had been in Thessalonica only three weeks. Was it possible to make such an impression on a place in three weeks' time that Christianity was planted so deeply that it could never again be uprooted? If so, it was by no means an idle dream that the Roman Empire might yet be won for Christ. Or was it necessary to settle down and work for months, even years, before an impression could be made? In that event, no man could even dimly foresee when Christianity would penetrate all over the world. Thessalonica was a test case; and Paul was torn with anxiety to know how it would turn out.

NEWS FROM THESSALONICA

So anxious was Paul that, when Timothy joined him at Athens, he sent him back to Thessalonica to get the information without which he could not rest (1 *Thessalonians* 3: 1, 2, 5; 2: 17). What news did Timothy bring back? There was good news. The affection of the Thessalonians for Paul was as strong as ever; and they were standing fast in the faith (1 *Thessalonians*

2: 14; 3: 4–6; 4: 9, 10). They were indeed "his glory and his joy" (1 *Thessalonians* 2: 20). But there was worrying news.

(i) The preaching of the Second Coming had produced an unhealthy situation in which people had stopped working and had abandoned all ordinary pursuits to await the Second Coming with a kind of hysterical expectancy. So Paul tells them to be quiet and to get on with their work (1 *Thessalonians* 4: 11).

(ii) They were worried about what was to happen to those who died before the Second Coming arrived. Paul explains that those who fall asleep in Jesus will miss none of the glory (1 *Thessalonians* 4: 13–18).

(iii) There was a tendency to despise all lawful authority; the argumentative Greek was always in danger of producing a democracy run mad (1 *Thessalonians* 5: 12–14).

(iv) There was the ever-present danger that they would relapse into immorality. It was hard to unlearn the point of view of generations and to escape the contagion of the heathen world (1 *Thessalonians* 4: 3–8).

(v) There was at least a section who slandered Paul. They hinted that he preached the gospel for what he could get out of it (1 *Thessalonians* 2: 5, 9); and that he was something of a dictator (1 *Thessalonians* 2: 6, 7, 11).

(vi) There was a certain amount of division in the Church (1 *Thessalonians* 4: 9; 5: 13).

These were the problems with which Paul had to deal; and they show that human nature has not changed so very much.

WHY TWO LETTERS?

We must ask why there are two letters. They are very much alike and they must have been written within weeks, perhaps days of each other. The second letter was written mainly to clear up a misconception about the Second Coming. The first letter insists that the Day of the Lord will come like a thief in the night, and urges watchfulness (1 *Thessalonians* 5: 2; 5: 6). But this produced the unhealthy situation where men did nothing but watch and wait; and in the second letter Paul explains what signs must come first before the Second Coming should come (2 *Thessalonians* 2: 3–12). The Thessalonians had got their ideas about the Second Coming out of proportion. As so often happens to a preacher, Paul's preaching had been misunderstood, and certain phrases had been taken out of context and over-emphasized; and the second letter seeks to put things back in their proper balance and to correct the thoughts of the excited Thessalonians regarding the Second Coming. Of course, Paul takes occasion in the second letter to repeat and to stress much of the good advice and rebuke he had given in the first, but its main aim is to tell them certain things which will calm their hysteria and make them wait, not in excited idleness, but in patient and diligent attendance to the day's work. In these two letters we see Paul solving the day to day problems which arose in the expanding Church.

1 THESSALONIANS

LOVE'S INTRODUCTION

1 *Thessalonians* 1

Paul and Silas and Timothy send this letter to the church of the Thessalonians which is in God the Father and the Lord Jesus Christ. Grace be to you and peace.

Always we thank God for you all and always we remember you in our prayers. We never cease to remember the work inspired by your faith, the labour prompted by your love and the endurance founded on your hope in our Lord Jesus Christ, before God who is also our Father. For we know, brothers beloved by God, how you were chosen. We know that our good news did not come to you with words only, but with power and with the Holy Spirit and with much conviction, just as you know what we showed ourselves to be to you for your sakes. And you became imitators of us and of the Lord, for although you received the word in much affliction, yet you received it with the joy of the Holy Spirit so that you became an example to all the believers in Macedonia and in Achaea. For the word of the Lord went forth from you like a trumpet, not only in Macedonia and Achaea, but the story of your faith towards God has gone forth in every place, so that we had no need to say anything about it. For the people amongst whom we were could tell us your story, and how we entered into you and how you turned from idols towards God, to serve the living and true God and to await the coming of his Son from heaven, even Jesus whom he raised from among the dead, and who rescues us from the coming wrath.

PAUL sends this letter to the church of the Thessalonians *which is in God and the Lord Jesus Christ*. God was the very atmosphere in which the Church lived and moved and had its being. Just as the air is in us and we are in the air and cannot live without it, so the true Church is in God and God is in the true Church and there is no true life for the Church without God. Further, the God in whom the Church lives is the God and Father of our Lord Jesus Christ; and, therefore, the Church does not shiver in the icy fear of a God who is a tyrant but basks in the sunshine of a God who is love.

In this opening chapter we see Paul at his most winsome. In a short time he was going to deal out warning and rebuke; but he begins with unmixed praise. Even when he rebuked, it was never his aim to discourage but always to uplift. In every man there is something fine, and often the best way to rid him of the lower things is to praise the higher things. The best way to eradicate his faults is to praise his virtues so that they will flower all the more; every man reacts better to encouragement then he does to rebuke. It is told that once the Duke of Wellington's cook gave notice and left him. He was asked why he had left so honourable and well-paid a position. His answer was, "When the dinner is good, the Duke never praises me and when it is bad, he never blames me; it was just not worth while." Encouragement was lacking. Paul, like a good psychologist and with true Christian tact, begins with praise even when he means to move on to rebuke.

In verse 3 Paul picks out three great ingredients of the Christian life.

(i) There is *work which is inspired by faith*. Nothing tells us more about a man than the way in which he works. He may work in fear of the whip; he may work for hope of gain; he may work from a grim sense of duty; or he may work inspired by faith. His faith is that this is his task given him by God and that he is working in the last analysis not for men but for God. Someone has said that the sign of true consecration is when a man can find glory in drudgery.

(ii) There is *the labour which is prompted by love*. Bernard Newman tells how once he stayed in a Bulgarian peasant's house. All the time he was there the daughter was stitching away at a dress. He said to her, "Don't you ever get tired of that eternal sewing?" "O no!" she said, "you see this is my wedding dress." Work done for love always has a glory.

(iii) There is *the endurance which is founded on hope*. When Alexander the Great was setting out on his campaigns, he divided all his possessions among his friends. Someone said, "But you are keeping nothing for yourself." "O yes, I am," he said. "I have kept my hopes." A man can endure anything so long as he has hope, for then he is walking not to the night, but to the dawn.

In verse 4 Paul speaks of the Thessalonians as *brothers beloved by God*. The phrase *beloved by God* was a phrase which the Jews applied only to supremely great men like Moses and Solomon, and to the nation of Israel itself. Now the greatest privilege of the greatest men of God's chosen people has been extended to the humblest of the Gentiles.

Verse 8 speaks of the faith of the Thessalonians sounding forth like *a trumpet*; the word could also mean crashing out like *a roll of thunder*. There is something tremendous about the sheer defiance of early Christianity. When all prudence would have dictated a way of life that would escape notice and so avoid danger and persecution, the Christians blazoned forth their faith. They were never ashamed to show whose they were and whom they sought to serve.

In verses 9 and 10 two words are used which are characteristic of the Christian life. The Thessalonians *served* God and *waited* on the coming of Christ. The Christian is called upon to serve in the world and to wait for glory. The loyal service and the patient waiting were the necessary preludes to the glory of heaven.

PAUL ON HIS DEFENCE

1 *Thessalonians* 2: 1–12

You yourselves know, brothers, that our coming among you was not to no effect; but after we had—as you know—already undergone suffering and ill-treatment at Philippi, we were bold in our God to tell you the good news of God, and a sore struggle we had. Our appeal to you did not proceed from any delusion, nor from impure motives, nor was it calculated to deceive; but as we have been deemed worthy by God to be entrusted with the good news, so we speak, not as if we were seeking to please men, but rather as if we were seeking to please God, who tests our hearts. At no time, as you know, did we use flattering words; at no time did we use our message as a pretext for greed; God is our witness; at no time did we seek reputation from men, either from you or from others, although we might well have claimed a place of weight, as apostles of Christ. But we showed ourselves gentle among you, treating you as a nurse cherishes her children. Yearning for you like this, we wanted to share with you, not only the good news of God, but even our very lives, because you had become very dear to us. For, brothers, you remember our labour and toil. It was while we were working night and day, so as not to be a burden to any of you, that we proclaimed the good news of God to you. You are our witnesses and so is God. How reverently and righteously and blamelessly we behaved to you who believed. As you know, as a father his children we exhorted and encouraged and solemnly charged each one of you to walk worthily of God who calls you to his Kingdom and his glory.

BENEATH the surface of this passage run the slanders which Paul's opponents at Thessalonica attached to him.

(i) Verse 2 refers to the imprisonment and abuse that he had received at Philippi (*Acts* 16: 16–40). There were, no doubt, those in Thessalonica who said that this man Paul had a police record, that he was nothing less than a criminal on the run from justice and that obviously no one should listen to a man like that. A really malignant mind will twist anything into a slander.

(ii) Verse 3 has behind it no fewer than three charges.

(*a*) It was being said that Paul's preaching came from sheer delusion. A really original man will always run the risk of being called mad. Festus thought that Paul was mad in later days (*Acts* 26: 24). There was a time when Jesus's friends came and tried to take him home because they thought that he was mad (*Mark* 3: 21). The Christian standards can be so different from the standards of the world that he who follows them with a single mind and a burning enthusiasm can appear to other men to be off his head.

(*b*) It was being said that Paul's preaching sprang from impure motives. The word used for *impurity* (*akatharsia*) often has to do with sexual impurity. There was one Christian custom which the heathen often and deliberately misinterpreted; that was the kiss of peace (1 *Thessalonians* 5:26). When the Christians spoke of the Love Feast and the kiss of peace, it was not difficult for an evil mind to read into these phrases what was never there. The trouble often is that a mind itself nasty will see nastiness everywhere.

(*c*) It was being said that Paul's preaching was guilefully aimed at deluding others. The propagandists of Hitler Germany discovered that if a lie is repeated often enough and loudly enough it will in the end be accepted as the truth. That was the charge which was levelled at Paul.

(iii) Verse 4 indicates that Paul was accused of seeking to please men rather than to please God. No doubt that rose from the fact that he preached the liberty of the gospel and the freedom of grace as against the slavery of legalism. There are always people who do not think that they are being religious unless they are being unhappy; and any man who preaches a gospel of joy will find his slanderers, which is exactly what happened to Jesus.

(iv) Verse 5 and verse 9 both indicate that there were those who said that Paul was in this business of preaching the gospel for what he could get out of it. The word used for *flattery* (*kolakeia*) always describes the flattery whose motive is gain. The trouble in the early Church was that there were people who did attempt to cash in on their Christianity. The first Christian book of order is called *The Didache, The Teaching of the Twelve Apostles,* and in it there are some illuminating instructions. "Let every apostle that cometh unto you be received as the Lord. And he shall stay one day and, if need be, the next also, but if he stay three days he is a false prophet. And when the apostle goeth forth, let him take nothing save bread, till he reach his lodging. But if he ask money, he is a false prophet." "No prophet that ordereth a table in the Spirit shall eat of it, else he is a false prophet." "If he that cometh is a passer-by, succour him as far as you can. But he shall not abide with you longer than two or three days unless there be necessity. But if he be minded to settle among you and be a craftsman, let him work and eat. But if he has no trade, according to your understanding, provide that he shall not live idle among you, being a Christian. But if he will not do this, he is a Christmonger: of such men beware." (*Didache,* chapters 11 and 12). The date of *The Didache* is about A.D. 100. Even the Early Church knew the perennial problem of those who traded on charity.

(v) Verse 6 indicates that Paul was accused of seeking personal prestige. It is the preacher's constant danger that he should seek to display himself and not the message. In 1 *Thessalonians* 1: 5 there is a suggestive thing. Paul does not say, "*I* came to you." He says, "*Our gospel* came to you." The man was lost in his message.

(vi) Verse 7 indicates that Paul was charged with being something of a dictator. His gentleness was that of a wise father. His was the love which knew how to be firm. To him Christian love was no easy sentimental thing; he knew that men needed discipline, not for their punishment but for the good of their souls.

THE SINS OF THE JEWS

1 *Thessalonians* 2: 13–16

> And for this, too, we thank God, that when you received the word of God which you heard from us, you accepted it, not as the word of men, but—as in truth it is—as the word of God, who also works in you who believe. For, brothers, you became imitators of the Churches of God which are in Judaea in Christ Jesus, for you too suffered the same things at the hands of your own fellow-countrymen as they did at the hands of the Jews; for they killed the Lord Jesus and the prophets, and they persecuted us, and they do not please God, and they are up against all men, and they try to stop us speaking to the Gentiles that they may be saved; and all this they keep on doing that they may complete the catalogue of their sins. But wrath to the uttermost has come upon them.

To the Thessalonians the Christian faith had brought not peace but trouble. Their new-found loyalty had involved them in persecution. Paul's method of encouraging them is very interesting. It is in effect to say to them,

> "Brothers, we are treading
>   Where the saints have trod."

Their persecution was a badge of honour which entitled them to rank with the picked regiments of the army of Christ.

But the great interest of this passage is that in verses 15 and 16 Paul draws up a kind of catalogue of the errors and the sins of the Jews.

(i) They killed the Lord Jesus and the prophets. When God's messengers came to them they eliminated them. One of the grim things about the gospel narrative is the intensity with which the leaders of the Jews sought to get rid of Jesus before he could do any more damage. But no man ever rendered a message inoperative by slaying the messenger who brought it. Someone tells of a missionary who went to a primitive tribe. He had to use primitive methods to get his message across; so he had a chart painted which showed the progress to heaven of the man who accepted Christ and the descent to hell of the man who rejected him. The message disturbed the tribe. They did not want it to be true. So *they burned the chart* and, having done so, thought all was well! A man may refuse to listen to the message of Jesus Christ but he cannot eliminate it from the structure of the universe.

(ii) They persecuted the Christians. Even although they themselves refused to accept the message of Christ, they might have allowed others to listen to it and, if they wished, to accept it. Let a man always remember that there are more ways to heaven than one; and let him keep himself from intolerance.

(iii) They did not try to please God. The Church's trouble has often been that it has clung to a man-made religion instead of a God-given faith. The question men have too often asked is, "What do I think?" instead of, "What does

God say?" It is not our puny logic that matters; it is God's revelation.

(iv) They were up against all men. In the ancient world the Jews were, in fact, accused of "hatred of the human race." Their sin was the sin of arrogance. They regarded themselves as the Chosen People, as indeed they were. But they regarded themselves as chosen for *privilege* and never dreamed that they were chosen for *service*. Their aim was that some day the world should serve them, not that at all times they should serve the world. The man who thinks only of his own rights and privileges will always be up against other men—and, what is more serious, he will be up against God.

(v) They wished to keep the offer of God's love exclusively to themselves and did not wish the Gentiles to have any share in his grace. Someone has summed up the exclusive attitude in four bitter lines of verse,

> "We are God's chosen few;
>   All others will be dammed.
>   There is no room in heaven for you;
>   We can't have heaven crammed."

There is something fundamentally wrong with a religion which shuts a man off from his fellow-men. If a man really loves God that love must run over into love for his fellow-men. So far from wanting to hug his privileges to himself, he will be filled with a passion to share them.

OUR GLORY AND OUR JOY

1 *Thessalonians* 2: 17–20

But, brothers, when we had been separated from you—in presence but not in heart—for a short time, we were the more exceedingly eager with a great desire to see your face. So we wished to come to you—I Paul longed for it once and again—but Satan blocked our way. For who is our hope or our joy or the crown in which we boast? Is it not even you, in the presence of the Lord Jesus Christ at his coming? For you are our glory and our joy.

FIRST Thessalonians has been called "a classic of friendship," and here is a passage where Paul's deep affection for his friends breathes through his words. Across the centuries we can still feel the throb of love in these sentences.

Paul uses two interesting pictures in this passage.

(i) He speaks of Satan *blocking his way* when he desired to come to Thessalonica. The word he uses (*egkoptein*) is the technical word for putting up a road-block calculated to stop an expedition on the march. It is Satan's work to throw obstacles into the Christian's way—and it is our work to surmount them.

(ii) He speaks of the Thessalonians being his *crown*. In Greek there are two words for *crown*. The one is *diadema* which is used almost exclusively for the royal crown. The other is *stephanos* which is used almost exclusively for the victor's crown in some contest and especially for the athlete's crown of victory in the games. It is *stephanos* that Paul uses here. The only prize in life that he really valued was to see his converts living well.

W. M. Macgregor used to quote the saying of John when he was thinking of the students whom he had taught, "No greater joy can I have than this, to hear that my children follow the truth." (3 *John* 4). Paul would have said amen to that. The glory of any teacher lies in his students; and should the day come when they have left him far behind the glory is still greater. A man's greatest glory lies in those whom he has set or helped on the path to Christ.

Anne Ross Cousin turned into verse the thoughts of Samuel Rutherford as he lay in prison in Aberdeen. In one verse she pictures him thinking of his old congregation in Anwoth:

> "Fair Anwoth on the Solway
> To me thou still art dear;
> Even from the verge of heaven
> I drop for thee a tear.

O! if one soul from Anwoth
Shall meet me at God's right hand,
My heaven will be two heavens
In Immanuel's land."

Nothing that we can do can bring us credit in the sight of God; but at the last the stars in a man's crown will be those whom he led nearer to Jesus Christ.

THE PASTOR AND HIS FLOCK

1 *Thessalonians* 3: 1–10

So, when we could not stand it any longer, we made up our minds to be left all alone in Athens, and we sent Timothy our brother and God's servant in the good news of Christ, to strengthen you and encourage you about your faith, to see that none of you is beguiled into leaving the faith because of these afflictions, for you yourselves know that that is the very work that God has appointed us to do. For, when we were with you, we told you beforehand that we Christians always suffer for our faith—as indeed it has turned out as you well know. So then, no longer able to stand it, I sent to find out how your faith is doing, in case the tempter had put you to the test and our labour should turn out to be all for nothing. But now that Timothy has come back to us from you, and has brought us the good news of your faith and love, and has told us that you always think kindly of us and that you always yearn to see us—just as we yearn to see you—because of this we have been encouraged, brothers, by you through your faith in all our straits and in all our afflictions, and because now life for us is indeed worth living if you stand fast in the Lord, what thanks can we return to God for you for all the joy with which we rejoice because of you before God, while night and day we keep on praying with all the intensity of our hearts to see your face and to fill up the gaps in your faith?

In this passage there breathes the very essence of the spirit of the pastor.

(i) There is *affection*. We can never affect or win people unless we begin, quite simply, by liking them. It was Carlyle who said of London, "There are three and a half million people in this city—mostly fools!" The man who begins by despising men or by disliking them can never go on to save them.

(ii) There is *anxiety*. When a man has put the best of himself into anything, when he has launched anything from a liner to a pamphlet, he is anxious until he knows how the work of his hands and of his brain will weather the storms. If that is true of things, it is still more poignantly true of people. When a parent has trained a child with love and sacrifice, he is anxious when that child is launched out on the difficulties and dangers of life in the world. When a teacher has taught a child and put something of himself into that teaching, he is anxious to see how that training will stand the test of life. When a minister has received a young person into the Church, after years of training in Sunday School and in Bible Class and latterly in the First Communicants' Class, in confirmation class, he is anxious to know how he will fulfil the duties and the obligations of Church membership. Supremely it is so with Jesus Christ. He staked so much on men and loved them with such a sacrificial love that he anxiously watches and waits to see how they will use that love. A man must stand awed and humbled when he remembers how in earth and in heaven there are those who are bearing him on their hearts and watching how he fares.

(iii) There is *help*. When Paul sent Timothy to Thessalonica it was not nearly so much to inspect the Church there as it was to help it. It should be the great aim of every parent, every teacher and every preacher, not so much to criticize and condemn those in his charge for their faults and mistakes but to save them from these faults and mistakes. The Christian attitude to the sinner and the struggler must never be that of condemnation but always that of help.

(iv) There is *joy*. Paul was glad that his converts were standing fast. He had the joy of one who had created something which would stand the tests of time. There is no joy like that of the parent who can point to a child who has done well.

(v) There is *prayer*. Paul carried his people on his heart to God's mercy seat. We will never know from how much sin we have been saved and how much temptation we have conquered all because someone prayed for us. It is told that once a servant-girl became a member of a Church. She was asked what Christian work she did. She said that she had not the opportunity to do much because her duties were so constant but, she said, "When I go to bed I take the morning newspaper to my bed with me; and I read the notices of the births and I pray for all the little babies; and I read the notices of marriage and I pray that those who have been married may be happy; and I read the announcements of death and I pray that the sorrowing may be comforted." No man can ever tell what tides of grace flowed from her attic bedroom. When we can serve people no other way, when, like Paul, we are unwillingly separated from them, there is one thing we can still do—we can pray for them.

ALL IS OF GOD

1 *Thessalonians* 3: 11–13

> May he who is our God and Father and the Lord Jesus Christ direct our way to you. May the Lord increase you and make you to abound in love to each other and to all men, even as we do towards you, in order that he may strengthen your hearts so that you may be blameless in holiness before the God who is our Father at the coming of our Lord Jesus with all his saints.

IT is in a simple passage like this that the instinctive turn of Paul's mind is best seen. For him everything was of God.

(i) He prays to God to open a way for him whereby he may come to Thessalonica. It was to God that he turned for guidance in the ordinary day to day problems of life. One of the great mistakes of life is to turn to God only in the overpowering emergencies and the shattering crises.

I remember once talking to three young men who had just completed a yachting expedition up the west coast of Scotland.

One said to me, "You know, when we are at home we hardly ever listen to the weather forecasts, but when we were on that yacht we listened to them with all our ears." It is quite possible to do without the weather forecasts when life is comfortably safe; it is essential to listen when life might depend on them.

We are apt to try to do the same with God. In ordinary things we disregard him, thinking that we can manage well enough by ourselves; in the emergency we clutch at him, knowing that we cannot get through without him. It was not so with Paul. Even in an ordinary routine thing like a journey from Athens to Thessalonica it was to God that he looked for guidance. We use him to try to achieve a God-rescued life; Paul companied with him to achieve a God-directed life.

(ii) He prays to God that he will enable the Thessalonians to fulfil the law of love in their daily lives. We often wonder why the Christian life is so difficult, especially in the ordinary everyday relationships. The answer may very well be that we are trying to live it by ourselves. The man who goes out in the morning without prayer is, in effect, saying, "I can quite well tackle today on my own." The man who lays himself to rest without speaking to God, is, in effect, saying, "I can bear on my own whatever consequences today has brought." John Buchan once described an atheist as "a man who has no invisible means of support." It may well be that our failure to live the Christian life well is due to our trying to live it without the help of God—which is an impossible assignment.

(iii) Paul prays to God for the ultimate safety. At this time his mind was full of thoughts of the Second Coming of Christ when men would stand before the judgment seat of God. It was his prayer that God would so preserve his people in righteousness that on that day they would not be ashamed. The only way to prepare to meet God is to live daily with him. The shock of that day will be not for those who have so lived that they have become God's friends but for those who meet him as a terrible stranger.

THE SUMMONS TO PURITY

1 *Thessalonians* 4: 1–8

> Finally then, brothers, we ask and urge you in the Lord Jesus,
> that, as you have received instructions from us as to how you
> must behave to please God, even so you do behave, that you may
> go on from more to more. For you know what orders we gave
> you through the Lord Jesus; for this is God's will for you, that you
> should live consecrated lives, I mean, that you should keep
> yourselves from fornication, that each of you should know how
> to possess his own body in consecration and in honour, not in
> the passion of lustful desire, like the Gentiles who do not know
> God, that in this kind of thing you should not transgress
> against your brother or try to take advantage of him. For of all
> these things the Lord is the avenger, as we have already told
> you and testified to you. For God did not call us to impurity but
> to consecration. Therefore he who rejects this instruction does not
> reject a man, but rejects the God who gives his holy Spirit to us.

IT may seem strange that Paul should go to such lengths
to inculcate sexual purity in a Christian congregation; but
two things have to be remembered. First, the Thessalonians
had only newly come into the Christian faith and they had
come from a society in which chastity was an unknown virtue;
they were still in the midst of such a society and the infection
of it was playing upon them all the time. It would be
exceedingly difficult for them to unlearn what they had for all
their lives accepted as natural. Second, there never was an age
in history when marriage vows were so disregarded and
divorce so disastrously easy. The phrase which we have
translated "that each of you should possess his own body
in consecration and in honour" could be translated, "that
each of you may possess his own *wife* in consecration and
in honour."

Amongst the Jews marriage was theoretically held in the
highest esteem. It was said that a Jew must die rather than
commit murder, idolatry or adultery. But, in fact, divorce
was tragically easy. The Deuteronomic law laid it down that

a man could divorce his wife if he found "some uncleanness" or "some matter of shame" in her. The difficulty was in defining what was a "matter of shame." The stricter Rabbis confined that to adultery alone; but there was a laxer teaching which widened its scope to include matters like spoiling the dinner by putting too much salt in the food; going about in public with her head uncovered; talking with men in the streets; speaking disrespectfully of her husband's parents in his presence; being a brawling woman (which was defined as a woman whose voice could be heard in the next house). It was only to be expected that the laxer view prevailed.

In Rome for the first five hundred and twenty years of the Republic there had not been a single divorce; but now under the Empire, as it has been put, divorce was a matter of caprice. As Seneca said, "Women were married to be divorced and divorced to be married." In Rome the years were identified by the names of the consuls; but it was said that fashionable ladies identified the years by the names of their husbands. Juvenal quotes an instance of a woman who had eight husbands in five years. Morality was dead.

In Greece immorality had always been quite blatant. Long ago Demosthenes had written: "We keep prostitutes for pleasure; we keep mistresses for the day-to-day needs of the body; we keep wives for the begetting of children and for the faithful guardianship of our homes." So long as a man supported his wife and family there was no shame whatsoever in extra-marital relationships.

It was to men and women who had come out of a society like that that Paul wrote this paragraph. What may seem to many the merest commonplace of Christian living was to them startlingly new. One thing Christianity did was to lay down a completely new code in regard to the relationship of men and women; it is the champion of purity and the guardian of the home. This can not be affirmed too plainly in our own day which again has seen a pronounced shift in standards of sexual behaviour.

In a book entitled *What I Believe*, a symposium of the basic beliefs of a selection of well-known men and women, Kingsley Martin writes: "Once women are emancipated and begin to earn their own living and are able to decide for themselves whether or not they have children, marriage customs are inevitably revised. 'Contraception,' a well-known economist once said to me, 'is the most important event since the discovery of fire.' Basically he was right, for it fundamentally alters the relations of the sexes, on which family life is built. The result in our day is a new sexual code; the old 'morality' which winked at male promiscuity but punished female infidelity with a life-time of disgrace, or even, in some puritanical cultures, with a cruel death, has disappeared. The new code tends to make it the accepted thing that men and women can live together as they will, but to demand marriage of them if they decide to have children."

The new morality is only the old immorality brought up-to-date. There is a clamant necessity in Britain, as there was in Thessalonica, to place before men and women the uncompromising demands of Christian morality, "for God did not call us to impurity but to consecration."

THE NECESSITY OF THE DAY'S WORK

1 *Thessalonians* 4: 9–12

You do not need that I should write to you about brotherly love; for you yourselves are taught of God to love one another. Indeed you do this very thing to all the brothers who are in the whole of Macedonia. But we do urge you, brothers, to go on to more and more, and to aim at keeping calm and minding your own business. We urge you to work with your hands, as we instructed you to do, so that your behaviour may seem to those outside the Church a lovely thing and so that you may need no one to support you.

THIS passage begins with praise but it ends in warning; and with the warning we come to the immediate situation behind the letter. Paul urged the Thessalonians to keep calm, to mind their own business and to go on working with their hands. The preaching of the Second Coming had produced an odd and awkward situation in Thessalonica. Many of the Thessalonians had given up their daily work and were standing about in excited groups, upsetting themselves and everybody else, while they waited for the Second Coming to arrive. Ordinary life had been disrupted; the problem of making a living had been abandoned; and Paul's advice was pre-eminently practical.

(i) He told them, in effect, that the best way in which Jesus Christ could come upon them was that he should find them quietly, efficiently and diligently doing their daily job. Principal Rainy used to say, "Today I must lecture; tomorrow I must attend a committee meeting; on Sunday I must preach; some day I must die. Well then, let us do as well as we can each thing as it comes to us." The thought that Christ will some day come, that life as we know it will end, is not a reason for stopping work; it is a reason for working all the harder and more faithfully. It is not hysterical and useless waiting but quiet and useful work which will be a man's passport to the Kingdom.

(ii) He told them that, whatever happened, they must commend Christianity to the outsider by the diligence and the beauty of their lives. To go on as they were doing, to allow their so-called Christianity to turn them into useless citizens, was simply to bring Christianity into discredit. Paul here touched on a tremendous truth. A tree is known by its fruits; and a religion is known by the kind of men it produces. The only way to demonstrate that Christianity is the best of all faiths is to show that it produces the best of all men. When we Christians show that our Christianity makes us better workmen, truer friends, kinder men and women, then we are really preaching. The outside world may never come into church to hear a sermon but it sees us every day outside church; and it is our lives which must be the sermons to win men for Christ.

(iii) He told them that they must aim at independence and never become spongers on charity. The effect of the conduct of the Thessalonians was that others had to support them. There is a certain paradox in Christianity. It is the Christian's duty to help others, for many, through no fault of their own, cannot attain that independence; but it is also the Christian's duty to help himself. There will be in the Christian a lovely charity which delights to give and a proud independence which scorns to take so long as his own two hands can supply his needs.

CONCERNING THOSE WHO ARE ASLEEP

1 *Thessalonians* 4: 13–18

We do not wish you to be ignorant, brothers, about those who are asleep, because we do not wish you to sorrow as the rest of people do because they have no hope. For if we believe that Jesus died and rose again, so also we can be sure that God will bring with him those who have fallen asleep through Jesus. For we tell you this, not by our own authority but by the word of the Lord, that we who are alive, who survive until the coming of the Lord, will certainly not take precedence over those who have fallen asleep. For the Lord himself will descend from heaven, with a shout of command, with the voice of an archangel and with the trumpet of God; and the dead who are in Christ will rise first, and then we who are alive, who survive, will be caught up by the clouds together with them to meet the Lord in the air. And so we shall be always with the Lord. So then encourage one another with these words.

THE idea of the Second Coming had brought another problem to the people of Thessalonica. They were expecting it very soon; they fully expected to be themselves alive when it came but they were worried about those Christians who had died. They could not be sure that those who had already died would share the glory of that day which was so soon to come.

Paul's answer is that there will be one glory for those who have died and those who survive.

He tells them that they must not sorrow as those who have no hope. In face of death the pagan world stood in despair. They met it with grim resignation and bleak hopelessness. Aeschylus wrote, "Once a man dies there is no resurrection." Theocritus wrote, "There is hope for those who are alive, but those who have died are without hope." Catullus wrote, "When once our brief light sets, there is one perpetual night through which we must sleep." On their tombstones grim epitaphs were carved. "I was not; I became; I am not; I care not." One of the most pathetic papyrus letters that has come down to us is a letter of sympathy which runs like this. "Irene to Taonnophris and Philo, good comfort. I was as sorry and wept over the departed one as I wept for Didymas. And all things whatsoever were fitting, I did, and all mine, Epaphroditus and Thermouthion and Philion and Apollonius and Plantas. But nevertheless against such things one can do nothing. Therefore comfort ye one another."

Paul lays down a great principle. The man who has lived and died in Christ is still in Christ even in death and will rise in him. Between Christ and the man who loves him there is a relationship which nothing can break, a relationship which overpasses death. Because Christ died and rose again, so the man who is one with Christ will rise again.

The picture Paul draws of the day when Christ will come is poetry, an attempt to describe what is indescribable. At the Second Coming Christ will descend from heaven to earth. He will utter the word of command and thereupon the voice of an archangel and the trumpet of God will waken the dead; then the dead and the living alike will be caught up in the chariots of the clouds to meet Christ; and thereafter they will be forever with their Lord. We are not meant to take with crude and insensitive literalism what is a seer's vision. It is not the details which are important. What is important is that in life and in death the Christian is in Christ and that is a union which nothing can break.

LIKE A THIEF IN THE NIGHT

1 *Thessalonians* 5: 1–11

You have no need, brothers, that anything should be written to you about the times and seasons; for you yourselves well know that, as a thief in the night, so the day of the Lord comes. When they are saying, "All is well; all is safe," then sudden destruction comes upon them, just as the labour pains come on a woman who is with child, and very certainly they will not escape. But you, brothers, are not in the dark. You are not in a situation in which the day, like a thief, can surprise you. For you are all sons of the light and sons of the day. We do not belong to night or darkness. So then, let us not sleep, as the rest of men do, but let us be watchful and sober. For those who sleep sleep at night; and those who get drunk get drunk at night; but, as for us, because we belong to the day, let us be sober and let us put on the breastplate of faith and love, and let us take for a helmet the hope of salvation, because God did not appoint us for wrath, but to obtain salvation through our Lord Jesus Christ, who died for our sins, so that, whether we wake or whether we sleep, we may live with him. So then encourage each other and build up one another—as indeed you are doing.

WE shall not fully understand the New Testament pictures of the Second Coming unless we remember that they have an Old Testament background. In the Old Testament the conception of the Day of the Lord is very common; and all the pictures and apparatus which belong to the Day of the Lord have been attached to the Second Coming. To the Jew all time was divided into two ages. There was this present age which was wholly and incurably bad. There was the age to come which would be the golden age of God. In between there was the Day of the Lord which would be a terrible day. It would be a day in which one world was shattered and another was born.

Many of the most terrible pictures in the Old Testament are of the Day of the Lord (*Isaiah* 22:5; 13:9; *Zephaniah* 1:14–16; *Amos* 5:18; *Jeremiah* 30:7; *Malachi* 4:1; *Joel* 2:31). Its main characteristics were as follows. (i) It would come suddenly and unexpectedly. (ii) It would involve a cosmic upheaval in which the universe was shaken to its very foundations. (iii) It would be a time of judgment.

Very naturally the New Testament writers to all intents and purposes identified the Day of the Lord with the day of the Second Coming of Jesus Christ. We will do well to remember that these are what we might call stock pictures. They are not meant to be taken literally. They are pictorial visions of what would happen when God broke into time.

Naturally men were anxious to know when that day would come. Jesus himself had bluntly said that no man knew when that day or hour would be, that even he did not know and only God knew (*Mark* 13: 32; cp. *Matthew* 24: 36; *Acts* 1: 7). But that did not stop people speculating about it, as indeed they still do, although it is surely almost blasphemous that men should seek for knowledge which was denied even to Jesus. To these speculations Paul has two things to say.

He repeats that the coming of the day will be sudden. It will come like a thief in the night. But he also insists that that is no reason why a man should be caught unawares. It is only the man who lives in the dark and whose deeds are evil who will be caught unprepared. The Christian lives in the light and no matter when that day comes, if he is watchful and sober, it will find him ready. Waking or sleeping, the Christian is living already with Christ and is therefore always prepared.

No man knows when God's call will come for him and there are certain things that cannot be left until the last moment. It is too late to prepare for an examination when the examination paper is before you. It is too late to make the house secure when the storm has burst. When Queen Mary of Orange was dying, her chaplain wished to read to her. She answered, "I have not left this matter till this hour." It was similar with an old Scotsman to whom someone offered comforting sayings near the end. The old man's reply was, "Ah theekit (thatched) ma hoose when the weather was warm." If a call comes suddenly, it need not find us unprepared. The man who has lived all his life with Christ is never unprepared to enter his nearer presence.

ADVICE TO A CHURCH

1 *Thessalonians* 5: 12–22

We ask you, brothers, to give due recognition to those who labour among you and to those who preside over you in the Lord and admonish you, and to hold them very highly in love because of the work that they are doing.

Be at peace among yourselves.
We urge you brothers, warn the lazy, comfort the fearful, cling to the weak, be patient with all
See that no one pays back evil for evil. Always pursue the good for each other and for all.
Always rejoice.
Never stop praying.
In everything give thanks.
For this is God's will in Christ Jesus for you.
Don't quench the gifts of the Spirit, don't make light of manifestations of the gift of prophecy.
Test everything, hold fast to the fine thing.
Keep yourselves well away from every kind of evil.

PAUL comes to an end with a chain of jewels of good advice. He sets them out in the most summary way but every one is such that every Christian should ponder it.

Respect your leaders, says Paul; and the reason for the respect is the work that they are doing. It is not a question of personal prestige; it is the task which makes a man great and it is the service he is doing which is his badge of honour.

Live at peace. It is impossible that the gospel of love should be preached in an atmosphere poisoned by hate Better far that a man should quit a congregation in which he is unhappy and in which he makes others unhappy and find one where he may be at peace.

Verse 14 picks out those who need special care and attention.

The word used for *lazy* originally described a soldier who had left the ranks. The phrase really means "Warn the quitters." The fearful are literally *those whose souls are small*. In every community there is the faint-hearted brother who instinctively fears the worst but in every community there should be Christians who, being brave, help others to be brave. "Cling to the weak" is a lovely piece of advice. Instead of letting the weak brother drift away and finally vanish altogether, the Christian community should make a deliberate attempt to grapple him to the Church in such a way that he cannot escape. It should forge bonds of fellowship and persuasion to hold on to the man who is likely to stray away. To be patient with all is perhaps hardest of all, for the last lesson most of us learn is to suffer fools gladly.

Don't take revenge, says Paul. Even if a man seeks our evil we must conquer him by seeking his good.

Verses 16–18 give us three marks of a genuine Church. (i) It is *a happy Church*. There is in it that atmosphere of joy which makes its members feel that they are bathed in sunshine. True Christianity is an exhilarating and not a depressing thing. (ii) It is *a praying Church*. Maybe our Church's prayers would be more effective if we remembered that "they pray best together who also pray alone." (iii) It is *a thankful Church*. There is always something for which to give thanks; even on the darkest day there are blessings to count. We must remember that if we face the sun the shadows will fall behind us but if we turn our backs on the sun all the shadows will be in front.

In verses 19 and 20 Paul warns the Thessalonians not to despise spiritual gifts. The prophets were really the equivalent of our modern preachers. It was they who brought the message of God to the congregation. Paul is really saying, "If a man has anything to say, don't stop him saying it."

Verses 21 and 22 describe the constant duty of the Christian. He must use Christ as touchstone by which to test all things; and even when it is hard he must keep on doing the fine thing and hold himself aloof from every kind of evil.

When a Church lives up to Paul's advice, it will indeed

shine like a light in a dark place; it will have joy within itself and power to win others.

THE GRACE OF CHRIST BE WITH YOU

1 Thessalonians 5: 23–28

May the God of peace himself consecrate you through and through; and may your spirit and soul and body be kept complete so that you will be blameless at the coming of our Lord Jesus Christ. You can rely on him who calls you—and he will do this very thing.

Brothers, pray for us.
Greet all the brothers with a holy kiss.
I adjure you by the Lord that this letter should be read to all the brothers.
The grace of our Lord Jesus Christ be with you.

AT the end of his letter Paul commends his friends to God in body, soul and spirit. But there is one very lovely saying here. "Brothers," said Paul, "pray for us." It is a wonderful thing that the greatest saint of them all should feel that he was strengthened by the prayers of the humblest Christians. Once his friends came to congratulate a great statesman who had been elected to the highest office his country could offer him. He said, "Don't give me your congratulations, but give me your prayers." For Paul prayer was a golden chain in which he prayed for others and others prayed for him.

2 THESSALONIANS

LIFT UP YOUR HEARTS

2 Thessalonians 1

Paul and Silas and Timothy send this letter to the Church of the Thessalonians which is in God our Father and the Lord Jesus Christ.

Brothers, we ought always to thank God for you, as it is fitting, because your faith is on the increase, and because the love of each one of you all for each other grows ever greater, so that we ourselves are telling proudly about you in the Churches of God, about your constancy and faith amidst all the persecutions and afflictions which you endure—which indeed is proof positive that the judgment of God was right that you should be deemed worthy of the Kingdom of God for the sake of which you are suffering. And just that judgment is, if indeed it is right in God's sight, as it is, to recompense affliction to those who afflict you and relief with us to you who are afflicted, when the Lord Jesus shall be revealed from heaven, with the power of his angels in a flame of fire when he renders a just recompense to those who do not recognize God and who do not obey the good news of our Lord Jesus. These are such men that they will pay the penalty of eternal destruction which will banish them forever from the face of the Lord and from the glory of his strength, when he shall come to be glorified in his saints and admired in all those who believed—because our testimony to you was believed—on that day. To this end we also always pray for you, that our God may deem you worthy of the call that came to you and that he may by his power bring to completion every resolve after goodness and every work that faith inspires, so that the name of our Lord Jesus may be glorified in you and you in it, according to the grace of our God and of the Lord Jesus Christ.

THERE is all the wisdom of the wise leader in this opening passage. It seems that the Thessalonians had sent a message to Paul full of self-doubtings. They had been timorously afraid that their faith was not going to stand the test and that—in the expressive modern phrase—they were not going to make the grade. Paul's answer was not to push them further into the slough of despond by pessimistically agreeing with them but to pick out their virtues and achievements in such a way that these despondent, frightened Christians might square their shoulders and say, "Well, if Paul thinks that of us we'll make a fight of it yet."

"Blessed are those," said Mark Rutherford, "who heal us of our self-despisings," and Paul did just that for the Thessalonian Church. He knew that often judicious praise can do what indiscriminate criticism cannot do and that wise praise never makes a man rest upon his laurels but fills him with the desire to do still better.

There are three things which Paul picked out as being the marks of a vital Church.

(i) *A faith which is strong.* It is the mark of the advancing Christian that he grows surer of Jesus Christ every day. The faith which may begin as an hypothesis ends as a certainty. James Agate once said, "My mind is not like a bed which has to be made and remade. There are some things of which I am absolutely sure." The Christian comes to that stage when to the thrill of Christian experience he adds the discipline of Christian thought.

(ii) *A love which is increasing.* A growing Church is one which grows greater in service. A man may begin serving his fellow-men as a duty which his Christian faith lays upon him; he will end by doing it because in it he finds his greatest joy. The life of service opens up the great discovery that unselfishness and happiness go hand in hand.

(iii) *A constancy which endures.* The word Paul uses is a magnificent word. It is *hupomone* which is usually translated *endurance* but does not mean the ability passively to bear anything that may descend upon us. It has been described as "a masculine constancy under trial" and describes the spirit which not only endures the circumstances in which it finds itself but masters them. It accepts the blows of life but in accepting them transforms them into stepping stones to new achievement.

Paul's uplifting message ends with the most uplifting vision of all. It ends with what we might call *the reciprocal glory*. When Christ comes he will be glorified *in his saints* and *admired in those who have believed.* Here we have the breath-taking truth that our glory is Christ and Christ's glory is ourselves. The glory of Christ is in those who through him have learned to endure and to conquer, and so to shine like lights in a dark place. A teacher's glory lies in the scholars he produces; a parent's in the children he rears not only for living but for life;

a master's in his disciples; and to us is given the tremendous privilege and responsibility that Christ's glory can lie in us. We may bring discredit or we may bring glory to the Master whose we are and whom we seek to serve. Can any privilege or responsibility be greater than that?

THE LAWLESS ONE

2 Thessalonians 2: 1–12

Brothers, in regard to the coming of our Lord Jesus Christ and in regard to our being gathered to him, we ask you not to be readily shaken in your mind and not to get into a state of nervous excitement because of any statement purporting to come from us either in the Spirit or by word of mouth or by a letter and alleging that the Day of the Lord is here. Let no one deceive you in any way. The Day of the Lord will not come unless there comes first The Rebellion against God, and unless there be revealed The Man of Sin, The Son of Perdition, the one who opposes himself to and exalts himself against everyone who is called God or made an object of worship so that he attempts to take his seat in the very temple of God and proclaims that he himself is God. Don't you remember that when I was still with you I told you these things? As for the present, you know the power which restrains him so that he may be revealed in his own time. For the secret of lawlessness is even now in operation. But The Man of Sin will appear only when the one who restrains him is removed from the scene. And then The Lawless One will be revealed and the Lord Jesus will destroy him with the breath of his mouth and will render him ineffective by his appearance and his coming. The coming of The Lawless One is for those who are doomed. He will come according to the working of Satan with all power and signs and wonders which issue from falsehood, and with all wicked deceit. They are doomed because they did not receive the love of truth that they might be saved. For this cause God sends them a deceiving energy in order that they might believe in a lie so that all who have not believed but have consented to that principle of unrighteousness may be judged.

THIS is undoubtedly one of the most difficult passages in the whole New Testament; and it is so because it is using terms and thinking in pictures which were perfectly familiar to those to whom Paul was speaking but which are utterly strange to us.

The general picture is this. Paul was telling the Thessalonians that they must give up their nervous, hysterical waiting for the Second Coming. He denied that he had ever said that the Day of the Lord had come. That was a misinterpretation of his words which must not be attributed to him; and he told them that before the Day of the Lord could come much had still to happen.

First there would come an age of rebellion against God; into this world there had already come a secret evil power which was working in the world and on men to bring this time of rebellion. Somewhere there was being kept one who was as much the incarnation of evil as Jesus was the incarnation of God. He was The Man of Sin, The Son of Perdition, The Lawless One. In time the power which was restraining him would be removed from the scene; and then this devil incarnate would come. When he came, he would gather his own people to him just as Jesus Christ had gathered his. Those who had refused to accept Christ were waiting to accept him. Then would come a last battle in which Christ would utterly destroy The Lawless One; Christ's people would be gathered to him and the wicked men who had accepted The Lawless One as their master would be destroyed.

We have to remember one thing. Almost all the Eastern faiths believed in a power of evil as they believed in a power of good; and believed, too, in a kind of battle between God and this power of evil. For instance, the Babylonians had a story that Tiamat, the dragon, had rebelled against Marduk, the creator, and had in the final battle been destroyed. Paul was dealing in a set of ideas which were common property. The Jews, too, had that idea. They called the Satanic power *Belial* or, more correctly, *Beliar*. When the Jews wished to describe a man as utterly bad they called him *a son of Beliar* (*Deuteronomy* 13: 13; 1 *Kings* 21: 10, 13; 2 *Samuel* 22: 5). In 2 *Corinthians* 6: 15 Paul uses this term as the opposite of God. This evil incarnate was the antithesis of God. The Christians took this over, later than Paul, under the title *Antichrist* (1 *John* 2: 18, 22; 4: 3). Obviously such a power cannot go on existing for ever in the universe; and there was widespread belief in a final battle in which God would triumph and this force of anti-God would be finally destroyed. That is the picture with which Paul is working.

What was the restraining force which was still keeping The Lawless One under control? No one can answer that question with certainty. Most likely Paul meant the Roman Empire. Time and again he himself was to be saved from the fury of the mob by the justice of the Roman magistrate. Rome was the restraining power which kept the world from insane anarchy. But the day would come when that power would be removed—and then would be chaos.

So then Paul pictures a growing rebellion against God, the emergence of one who was the devil incarnate as Christ had been God incarnate, a final struggle and the ultimate triumph of God.

When this incarnate evil came into the world there would be some who would accept him as master, those who had refused Christ; and they along with their evil master would find final defeat and terrible judgment.

However remote these pictures may be from us they nevertheless have certain permanent truth in them.

(i) There is a force of evil in the world. Even if he could not logically prove that there was a devil many a man would say, "I know there is because I have met him." We hide our heads in the sand if we deny that there is an evil power at work amongst men.

(ii) God is in control. Things may seem to be crashing to chaos but in some strange way even the chaos is in God's control.

(iii) The ultimate triumph of God is sure. In the end nothing can stand against him. The Lawless One may have his day but there comes a time when God says, "Thus far and no farther." And so the great question is, "On what side are you? In the struggle at the heart of the universe are you for God—or Satan?"

GOD'S DEMAND AND OUR EFFORT

2 Thessalonians 2: 13–17

> We ought always to give thanks for you, brothers beloved by the Lord, because God chose you from the beginning to be saved by the consecration of the Holy Spirit and by faith in the truth. For this he called you by the good news which we brought, that you might obtain the glory of our Lord Jesus Christ. So then, brothers, stand fast and hold on to the traditions which you were taught either by word of mouth or through our letter.
>
> May the Lord Jesus Christ himself and God our Father, who loved us and who gave us, by his grace, eternal encouragement and good hope, encourage your hearts and make you strong in every good deed and word

In this passage there is a kind of synopsis of the Christian life.

(i) It begins with God's call. We could never even begin to seek God unless he had already found us. The whole initiative is with him; the ground and the moving cause of the whole matter is his seeking love

(ii) It develops in our effort. The Christian is not called to dream, but to fight; not to stand still, but to climb. He is called not only to the greatest privilege but also to the greatest task in the world.

(iii) This effort is helped continually by two things. (*a*) It is helped by the teaching, guidance and example of godly men. God speaks to us through those to whom he has already spoken. "A saint," as someone has said, "is a person who makes it easier for others to believe in God." And there are some who help us, not by anything they say or write, but simply by being what they are, men whom to meet is to meet God. (*b*) It is helped by God himself. We are never left to fight and toil alone. He who gives us the task also gives us the strength to do it; more, he actually does it with us. We are not thrown into the battle to meet it with the puny resources we can bring to it. At the back of us and beside us there is God. When Paul was up against it in Corinth, he had a vision by night in which the Lord said to him, "Do not be afraid . . . for I am with

You" (*Acts* 18: 9, 10). They that are for us are always more than they that are against us.

(iv) This call and this effort are designed to produce two things. (*a*) They are designed to produce *consecration on earth*. Literally in Greek a thing which is consecrated is *set apart for God*. They are meant to set us apart in such a way that God can use us for his service. The result is that a man's life no longer belongs to him to do with it as he likes; it belongs to God for *him* to use as he likes. (*b*) They are designed to produce *salvation in heaven*. The Christian life does not end with time; its goal is eternity. The Christian can regard his present affliction as a light thing in comparison with the glory that shall be. As Christina Rosetti wrote:

" 'Does the road wind uphill all the way?'
  'Yes, to the very end.'
'Will the day's journey take the whole long day?'
  'From morn to night, my friend.'

'But is there for the night a resting-place?'
  'A roof for when the slow dark hours begin.'
'May not the darkness hide it from my face?'
  'You cannot miss that inn.'

'Shall I meet other wayfarers at night?'
  'Those who have gone before.'
'Then must I knock, or call when just in sight?'
  'They will not keep you waiting at that door.'

'Shall I find comfort, travel-sore and weak?'
  'Of labour you shall find the sum.'
'Will there be beds for me and all who seek?'
  'Yes, beds for all who come.' "

A FINAL WORD

2 Thessalonians 3: 1–5

Finally, brothers, keep on praying for us, that the word of God may run its race and receive its crown of glory—as it does in your case—and that we may be saved from these wicked and evil men, for the faith is not for everyone. You can rely on the Lord who will make you steady and who will guard you from the evil one. We have confidence in the Lord that you both do and will do what we command you to do. May the Lord direct your hearts so that you may feel the love of God and display the endurance which Christ can give.

ONCE again Paul comes to the end of a letter with the request that his people should pray for him (cp. 1 *Thessalonians* 5: 25; *Romans* 15: 30 ff.; *Philemon* 22). There is something deeply moving in the thought of this giant among men asking for the prayers of the Thessalonians who so well recognized their own weakness. Nowhere is Paul's humility more clear to see. And the fact that he, as it were, threw himself on their hearts must have done much to bind even his opponents to him, because it is very difficult to dislike a man who asks you to pray for him.

But in spite of his love for and trust in men Paul was a realist. The faith, he said, is not for everyone. We can be certain that he said it not cynically but sorrowfully. Once again we see the tremendous responsibility of free-will. We can use it to open our hearts and we can use it to shut them. Faith's appeal is not selective, it goes out to every man; but the heart of man can refuse to respond.

In the last verse of this passage we see what we might call the inward and the outward characteristics of the Christian. The inward characteristic is the awareness of the love of God, the deep awareness that we cannot drift beyond his care, the sense that the everlasting arms are underneath us. One of the basic needs of life is security and we find that need met in the consciousness of the unchanging love of God. The outward characteristic is the endurance which Christ can give. We live in a world where there are more nervous breakdowns than at any time in history. It is a sign that more and more people have the feeling that they cannot cope with life. The outward characteristic of the Christian is that when others break he stands erect and when others collapse he shoulders his burden and goes on. With the love of God in his heart and the strength of Christ in his life a man can face anything.

DISCIPLINE IN BROTHERLY LOVE

2 *Thessalonians* 3 · 6–18

> Brothers, we command you in the name of our Lord Jesus Christ, keep yourselves from every brother who behaves like a truant from duty and who does not conduct himself in accordance with the teaching which they received from us, for you yourselves know that you must imitate us because we never played the truant from work when we were among you nor did we eat bread which we had received from you without paying for it, but in labour and toil we kept on working night and day so that we would not be a burden to any of you. It is not that we had not the right to claim support from you, but we kept at work that we might give ourselves to you as an example for you to imitate, for when we were with you we used to give you this order, "If a man refuses to work, neither let him eat." For we hear that there are some amongst you whose behaviour is that of truants from work, who are busy in nothing except in being busybodies To such we give orders and exhort them in the Lord Jesus Christ that they should quietly go on working and so eat their bread. Brothers, don't grow tired of doing the fine thing. If anyone does not obey the word we send to you through this letter, mark him; don't associate with him that he may be shamed. Don't reckon him as an enemy, but give him advice as a brother.
>
> May the Lord of peace himself give you peace always and everywhere. The Lord be with you all
>
> Here is the greeting of me Paul in my own hand-writing, which is the sign of genuineness in every letter. This is how I write. The grace of our Lord Jesus Christ be with you all.

HERE Paul is dealing, as he had to deal in the previous letter, with the situation produced by those who took the wrong attitude to the Second Coming. There were those in Thessalonica who had given up their work and had abandoned the routine claims of every day to wait about in excited idleness for Christ to come. Paul uses a vivid word to describe them. Twice he uses the adverb *ataktos* and once the verb *ataktein*. The word means *to play truant*. It occurs, for instance, in the papyri, in an apprentice's contract in which the father agrees that his son must make good any days on which he plays truant. The Thessalonians in their excited idleness were truants from work.

To bring them to their senses Paul quotes his own example. All his life he was a man who worked with his hands. The Jew glorified work. "He who does not teach his son a trade," they said, "teaches him to steal." Paul was a trained Rabbi; but the Jewish law laid it down that a Rabbi must take no pay for teaching. He must have a trade and must satisfy his daily needs with the work of his hands. So we find Rabbis who were bakers, barbers, carpenters, masons and who followed all kinds of trades. The Jews believed in the dignity of honest toil; and they were sure that a scholar lost something when he became so academic and so withdrawn from life that he forgot how to work with his hands. Paul quotes a saying, "If a man refuses to work, neither let him eat." It is the *refusal* to work that is important. This has nothing to do with the unfortunate man who, through no fault of his own, can find no work to do. This has been called "the golden rule of work." Deissmann has the happy thought that, when Paul said this, "he was probably borrowing a bit of good old workshop morality, a maxim coined perhaps by some industrious workman as he forbade his lazy apprentice to sit down to dinner."

In this we have the example of Jesus himself. He was the carpenter of Nazareth and legend has it that he made the best ox-yokes in all Palestine and that men came from all over the country to buy them. A tree is known by its fruits and a man is known by his work. Once a man was negotiating to buy a house and bought it without even seeing it. He was asked why he took such a risk; his answer was, "I know the man who built that house and he builds his Christianity in with the bricks." The Christian should be a more conscientious work-man than anyone else.

Paul disliked the busybody intensely. There may be greater sins than gossip but there is none which does more damage in the Church. A man who is doing his own work with his whole strength will have enough to do without being maliciously interested in the affairs of others.

Paul commands that those who disregard his instructions must be dealt with by the community. But they are to be dealt with not as enemies but as brothers. The discipline given by a man who contemptuously looks down upon the sinner and speaks to hurt may terrify and wound but it seldom amends. It is more likely to produce resentment than reformation. When Christian discipline is necessary it is to be given as by a brother to a brother, not in anger, still less in contempt but always in love.

At the end Paul adds his autograph to authenticate his letter. "Look," he says, "this is what my handwriting is like. Mark it, so that you will know it again." And then, with the truth expounded, with praise and rebuke lovingly intermingled, he commends the Thessalonian Church to the grace of the Lord Jesus Christ.

FURTHER READING

Philippians

J. B. Lightfoot, *Saint Paul's Epistle to the Philippians* (MmC; *G*)
R. P. Martin, *The Epistle of Paul to the Philippians* (TC; *E*)
J. H. Michael, *The Epistle of Paul to the Philippians* (MC; *E*)
M. R. Vincent, *Philippians and Philemon* (ICC; *G*)

Colossians

T. K. Abbott, *Ephesians and Colossians* (ICC; *G*)
J. B. Lightfoot, *St Paul's Epistles to the Colossians and Philemon* (MmC; *G*)
C. F. D. Moule, *The Epistles of Paul the Apostle to the Colossians and to Philemon* (CGT; *G*)
E. F. Scott, *The Epistles to Colossians, Philemon and Ephesians* (MC; *E*)

Thessalonians

J. E. Frame, *Thessalonians* (ICC; *G*)
G. Milligan, *St Paul's Epistles to the Thessalonians* (MmC; *G*)
W. Neil, *The Epistles of Paul to the Thessalonians* (MC; *E*)

Abbreviations

CGT : Cambridge Greek Testament
ICC : International Critical Commentary
MC : Moffatt Commentary
MmC: Macmillan Commentary
TC : Tyndale Commentary

E : English Text
G : Greek Text